WALKING LONDON'S
STATUES AND MONUMENTS

obvious and readily understandable correlation between times of national confidence, wealth and success, and the physical manifestation of those characteristics by way of the ornamentation of London's streets. The fact that London has maintained such a varied historic collection of statuary, with a good few relative villains among the commemorated, is also a mark of a city that is at ease with itself and with its history.

Aesthetics

These public ornaments are not just for commemoration. You will see a few aesthetic horrors (although everyone will have their own reaction to each piece), but also many more extraordinarily distinguished works of sculptural art. Recurring names of sculptors on these walks are Westmacott, Chantry and Boehm, all of the nineteenth century; Brock, Frampton, Gilbert and Thornycroft, all straddling the nineteenth and twentieth centuries; and Reid Dick, Epstein, Paolozzi and Wheeler, all of the twentieth century. Among architects who have designed either monuments themselves or the sites, in one form or another, for public sculpture are Wren, Taylor, Barry, Tite, two Gilbert Scotts, Lutyens, Baker, Webb and Blomfield. What that brief selection of names has in common is that every one of them was knighted, which is one small measure of the prominence and status of these creators of the capital's public ornamentation.

The decorative function of public sculpture has always been an important purpose of every work, even where the primary purpose has obviously been commemoration. The most conspicuous illustration of that duality on any of these walks is the Albert Memorial, with Albert's memory lauded, almost literally, to the skies, and in the most opulent High Victorian Gothic splendour. But the decorative element is perhaps more interesting in the non-commemorative work. A progression, or regression, if you prefer, has occurred: from the baroque to the postmodern, from the sculptural embellishment of buildings that are themselves already ornate, to rather starker and more functional buildings with the decorative sculptural role transferred to free-standing works. Contrast the facade of the west end of St Paul's Cathedral, or the complex allegorical adornment of the pediments of the Mansion House, the British Museum and the Royal Exchange, for example, through the more subordinate but still integral decoration of the early twentieth-century Bank of England by Wheeler or of various buildings by Epstein, to the separate free-standing sculptural enhancement of modern developments like Broadgate and Ludgate in the City, and of course Canary Wharf. In one sense, that change is hardly surprising, since so much of modern commercial architecture involves glass and steel. An extreme example like the Gherkin – the lozenge-shaped Swiss Re building in the City – simply does not admit sculptural embellishment. What is encouraging, though, is the extent of the enduring enlightenment and philanthropy that continues to promote London's public sculpture, decorative as well as commemorative. Perhaps the most conspicuous examples of this that these walks will visit are in Broadgate and Canary Wharf.

The materials of the sculptural works themselves, on the other hand, have been rather more consistent than the materials of the buildings that they have adorned, or by which they have been surrounded. The walks include a number of works in marble, but more often than not those are works that have not weathered well. You will find a greater number in stone, generally Portland stone, and particularly where the sculptures are integral parts of buildings. A much smaller number of modern works are in granite or stainless steel, and older works in lead. Almost uniquely, at least on these walks, Eros at Piccadilly is in aluminium, since any heavier metal would have made the balance of the work a physical impossibility.

For the free-standing statuary, by far the most common medium is bronze: the alloy of copper and tin has been known to man for several thousand years; molten bronze requires a relatively low working temperature; and bronze artefacts, whether cannons or coins, spears or statues, are remarkably durable. Some of the bronze statues on these walks have acquired a very dark, dull, dirty patina – the unloved Whig pair by Westmacott at either end of Bedford Place, for example – but the decay is only skin-deep and is reversible. The mounted bronze of Charles I at Charing Cross, now nearly four hundred years old, has just been cleaned and looks as good as new. The much cleaner air in London since the 1950s has greatly helped the preservation of public statuary, of course, particularly in stone. Most of the works seen on these walks could pretty much last for ever.

The Cost

Indeed, those who have commissioned public sculpture over the years have doubtless been extremely keen that their purchases should last a long time. Even a modest half life-size bronze will cost today several thousand pounds merely for its casting, quite apart from the fee of the sculptor. Most public bronzes are substantially larger than life-size, for obvious reasons, and those that you see on these walks will tend to be the work of distinguished sculptors whose fees would not have been by any means negligible. By way of random examples – all being statues that are included on these walks: Charles I, at Charing Cross, in 1633 cost £600; Queen Anne, eighty years later, nearly £1,200; Pitt in 1831, under the hand of Chantrey, the leading portrait sculptor of his day, £7,000; the Albert Memorial in the 1870s, the then colossal sum of over £100,000; Haig, in Whitehall, in 1937, £9,000; Roosevelt in 1948, £40,000; and Mountbatten in 1983, £100,000. Those are all contemporary sums, to which the appropriate historic inflationary multiplier must be applied.

Far more often than not, the cost of commemorative sculpture is met privately, or by subscription. Parliament voted £50,000 towards the huge cost overrun of the Albert Memorial and paid for Haig in his entirety (the plinth bearing the words 'Erected by Parliament'), but those were rare exceptions. While public subscription paid for the whole of Presidents Roosevelt and Kennedy, and half of Lord Mountbatten, private donations, collections and subscriptions tend to be the usual way of financing these works.

Non-commemorative works are a little different. Where the works are an integral part of the buildings to which they are attached, on the whole they are the product of enlightened patronage, whether of the Church, or the Corporation of London, or the Court of the Bank of England, or even – amazing to contemplate today – the directors of London Transport, with their embellishment of 55 Broadway. The same enlightened philanthropy can reasonably be attributed, at least in part, to a number of modern property developers, Rosehaugh Stanhope at Broadgate and Olympia & York at Canary Wharf being conspicuous examples. It is also an aspect of property development that forms part of the peripheral negotiations between developers and planning authorities. What 'planning gain' can be generated for the community at large, in return for granting permission for a particular project? Certainly public sculpture is on the 'planning gain' menu, several million pounds for sculptural embellishment being a relatively modest addition to the several hundreds of millions of pounds that a scheme like Broadgate cost.

About the Walks

This book describes thirteen walks, with a historical and anecdotal commentary on the statuary and monuments encountered on them. It is not a comprehensive record of all the public sculpture in central London, far from it. Although the walks are of differing lengths, each one is intended to be manageably short while at the same time including a reasonably dense concentration of interesting sculpture, and those two criteria pretty much by themselves define the book's geographical scope: the City, Bloomsbury, the West End, the central Embankment, the West End parks and Belgravia. Even within those parameters, however, the book covers a lot of ground, from Liverpool Street in the east to Kensington Palace in the west, and from Euston in the north to Victoria in the south, or in terms of the river, from Battersea to Greenwich. There are well over four hundred works included in the thirteen walks.

The approximate time it takes to complete the route is given at the beginning of each walk. Even the two longest walks – the first, round Hyde Park and Kensington Gardens, and the last, embracing Canary Wharf and Greenwich – are not going to occupy the gentle stroller for more than a morning or afternoon, while a mere 45 minutes will suffice for the shortest, from Parliament Square up Whitehall. Although the broad thrust of the book is from west to east, the walks are not consecutive. A route map accompanies the text. Each walk begins at an Underground station, for convenience, but otherwise is entirely self-contained. The closest Underground station to the end of the route is shown on the map and the route to it described in the text.

Although the most conspicuous and numerous of the works that you will see will be free-standing statues, there are plenty of other sculptural and monumental works to view. It seemed both incomplete and illogical to inform you about the free-standing statuary but to ignore, for example, monuments like the Monument itself, the Cenotaph and the Eleanor Cross, and sculpture as varied as the modern pieces at Broadgate, the embellishments of 55 Broadway by Epstein and others, and the pediments of the Mansion House and the Royal Exchange. And besides, John Betjeman's exhortation 'Don't look at shopfronts, look above them' yields plenty of sculptural fruit, as well as the buildings themselves. Nevertheless, an abiding limitation throughout the book is that these are all public outdoor works that can be seen without restriction at any time, with the rare odd exception.

Notes

• Each sculptural work appears in bold type and with a number: the same number identifies the location of that work on the relevant map.

• Each sculptor and architect appears in italics. Both the sculptural works and the sculptors and architects (with their correct titles) are listed alphabetically in the two indices at the end (see pages 142–59).

• 'Pevsner' refers to the relevant current volumes of Sir Nikolaus Pevsner's *The Buildings of England.*

• *ODNB* is the *Oxford Dictionary of National Biography.*

• A note of caution: London's public statuary can be remarkably mobile and sometimes elusive: pieces are displaced or hidden by building works or shifted altogether. They are removed for cleaning and repair. This book is a present-day snapshot and not a record cast, as it were, in stone.

Walking London's Statues and Monuments

Kilburn

Camden Town

Primrose Hill

Penton

Maida Vale

The West End p.64

Bloomsbury p.110

Clerker

Marylebone

Bloomsbury

Holb

City Approaches p.82

Notting Hill

Five Squares and a Circus p.54

Hyde Park and Kensington Gardens p.14

The Embankment p.73

Kensington

St James's Park p.34

Knightsbridge

Lamb

Belgravia p.25

Brompton

Belgravia

Parliament and Whitehall p

Westminster

Chelsea

Pimlico

Pimlico and Chelsea Embankments p.120

Fulham

Putney

Clapham

N

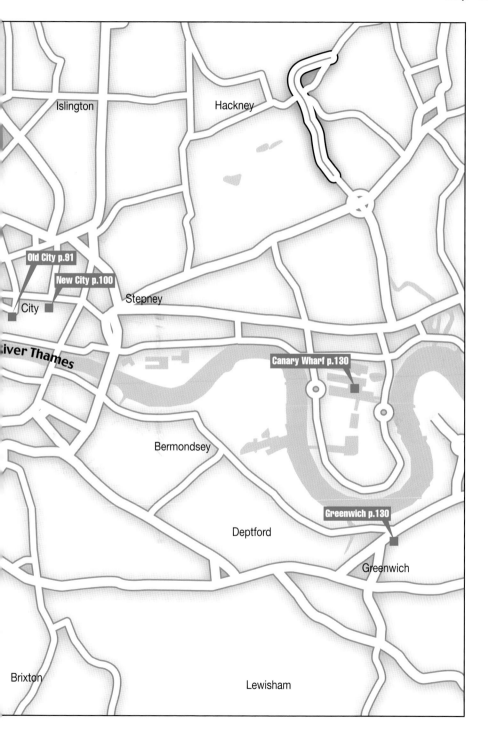

Islington

Hackney

Old City p.91

New City p.100

City

Stepney

River Thames

Canary Wharf p.130

Bermondsey

Greenwich p.130

Deptford

Greenwich

Brixton

Lewisham

1. HYDE PARK AND KENSINGTON GARDENS – FROM MARBLE ARCH TO THE ALBERT MEMORIAL

START	Marble Arch Underground Station (Central line)
FINISH	High Street Kensington Underground Station (Circle and District lines)
DISTANCE	9.5 km (6 miles)
DURATION	2 ½ hours

Right at the heart of London, the combination of Hyde Park and Kensington Gardens provides a huge, green, open public space extending more than 2.4 km (1 ¹/₂ miles) from east to west and 1.2 km (3/4 mile) from north to south. Hyde Park comprises over 140 hectares (346 acres) of open parkland and 4,000 trees, and Kensington Gardens add another 110 hectares (272 acres). To put these areas in an international context, Central Park in New York comprises 340 hectares (840 acres) and the Jardins des Tuileries in Paris a mere 25 hectares (62 acres). With the exceptions of the small formal gardens at either end of the lake dividing the park and gardens, all the landscaping is informal and very English. Apart from buildings like the Hilton Hotel and the Household Cavalry barracks, there are no high-rise buildings adjoining this vast green oasis and therefore few urban breaks in the treeline view from the middle.

Nowadays there is no practical distinction between the park and gardens and both fall within the domain of the Royal Parks. This first walk, the longest in the book, begins in the north-east corner of the park and ends, after considerable meandering, in the south-west corner of the gardens.

History of the Park and Gardens

Hyde Park was first acquired and enclosed by Henry VIII for hunting in 1536. It has been a Royal Park ever since. It was still used as a hunting ground well into the eighteenth century, but even before the end of the seventeenth century, after the Restoration, it had become a place for fashionable promenading. Rotten Row (said to be a corruption of Route du Roi, or King's Road, the broad carriageway along the south side of the park) was first laid out in 1690. Originally part of William III's carriage drive from Whitehall to Kensington Palace, it was designated a public bridleway in the 1760s and later became the first lamplit road in Britain.

Kensington Gardens were formerly the private gardens of Kensington Palace. A relatively modest country house in the seventeenth century, Kensington House (as it then was) was acquired by William III and Queen Mary in 1689. It was substantially enlarged and embellished by them and subsequently also under Queen Anne and George I. The principal architect involved was the most famous of all English architects, *Christopher Wren*, surveyor-general of the Royal Works for half a century from 1668. The main surviving landscaping also dates from the reign of George I, particularly the Great Basin (now known as the Round Pond) immediately to the east of the palace and the three principal avenues leading towards Hyde Park.

The defining feature of the park and gardens is the huge lake that runs roughly from north-west to south-east through the middle of the informal landscaping. The north-western end, within Kensington Gardens, is called Long Water, while the larger part to the east of the road bridge bears the better-known name, the Serpentine. The lake was created in 1731 at the instigation of Queen Caroline, George II's consort, by linking a series of pools fed by the Westbourne Brook from the north and building a dam at the south-east end.

Marble Arch

Exit Marble Arch Underground Station via the Hyde Park exit (subway 3). You will find yourself at **Marble Arch [1]**. It is effectively marooned on a traffic island and is rather unloved and largely unvisited. It is clad in white Carrara marble and its design owes much to the Arch of Constantine, beside the Coliseum in Rome, and to the Arc du Carrousel, by the Louvre in Paris. Like the Wellington Arch at Hyde Park Corner, it does not stand on its original site, having been designed by *John Nash* in 1825–6 as a gateway for Buckingham Palace, where it was first erected. When the palace forecourt was enclosed in 1851, the arch was moved and re-erected here at the junction of the great Roman roads to the west and north-west. This was also the site of Tyburn, where public executions took place as late as 1783. The site is discreetly marked on the traffic island at the bottom of Edgware Road. Road layout changes in 1908 and again in 1961 have left the arch on its present island site. The ornamentation of the arch was never completed and although the north and south sides bear sculptural decoration by *Richard Westmacott* and *Edward Hodges Baily* respectively, other proposed adornments were used elsewhere. The most notable example is the equestrian statue of **George IV**, which now stands in Trafalgar Square rather than on top of the arch (you can see this statue if you complete the walk on pages 54–63). The central gateway, with its bronze gates by *Samuel Parker*, is rarely used other than by the King's Troop of the Royal Horse Artillery, which rides down from its barracks in Marylebone to fire occasional ceremonial salutes in the park. The arch's three rooms once housed one of the smallest police stations in the world, but the station was closed in 1950.

Raoul Wallenberg

Cross the road on the north side of the arch to get a better view of its other side, then take a very brief diversion up Great Cumberland Place before beginning your walk in the park. You will be amply repaid by *Philip Jackson's* 1997 bronze of **Raoul Wallenberg [2]** outside the Western Marble Arch Synagogue (32 Great Cumberland Place). Swedish diplomat and Righteous Gentile, heroic and tragic, Wallenberg saved possibly over one hundred thousand Hungarian Jews from Nazi death camps, before himself being arrested by the victorious Red Army in 1945 and disappearing without trace into the Soviet Gulag system. The statue depicts Wallenberg standing against a wall constructed of the thousands of *schutzpasses*, or protective passports, which he issued to refugees so that they had Swedish diplomatic protection. The statue was unveiled on 26 February 1997 by The Queen, in the presence of the President of Israel and the then UN secretary-general, Kofi Annan, whose wife is Wallenberg's niece.

Along Park Lane

Part of Marble Arch's relative isolation can be laid at the door of the London County Council's road improvements in 1961, when Park Lane was made into a dual carriageway and a large swathe was chopped off the east side of Hyde Park, whose old boundary is the line of trees now standing in the central reservation between the carriageways. Walk down the west side of Park Lane and at the Brook Gate intersection you will find the **Animals in War Memorial [3]** by *David Backhouse*, which was unveiled by the Princess Royal in 2004. Stand on the south side of the memorial and you will face two concave curved stone panels. On the right there is an inscribed dedication and on the left various pack animals in relief, in particular a majestic elephant. Two bronze artillery pack mules walk towards the cleft in the stone panels and beyond the cleft on the north side are bronzes of a dog and a horse. The animals are all well executed, the pack mules are particularly effective, but there is something inescapably mawkish about the overall concept of an animal memorial.

Return to the west side of Park Lane, enter Hyde Park and walk a short distance south down the Broad Walk to Grosvenor House, where (branching off to your left) you will find **The Joy of Life Statue and Fountain [4]**, a large water feature by *T. B. Huxley-Jones* in 1963. This occupies what was previously the site of the Boy and Dolphin Fountain, which was moved to Regent's Park in 1962 but returned in 1994 to another site in Hyde Park (you will see it later in the walk). Two large (one male, one female, both ethnically neutral to the point of blandness) and four smaller bronze figures gambol,

in a rather surprisingly joyless manner, in the basins of this tribute to the joy of life. It is such a shame that this fountain and most other public fountains in London have no running water. A thousand miles south, every fountain in Rome gushes liberally – so why not in London?

Continue south down Lover's Walk from **The Joy of Life Statue**. When you are almost parallel with the Hilton Hotel, a broad gravel path runs away to your left, towards Park Lane, and leads to the 52 pillars, or 'stellae', of rough textured stainless steel which comprise the **7/7 Memorial [5]**, the memorial to the victims of the four terrorist atrocities which occurred in London on 7 July 2005, when 52 people were killed and many more were injured by suicide bombers on London's transport system. The pillars are grouped in four interlocking clusters reflecting the four terrorist attacks, each pillar bearing an inscription of the date and location of the attack represented by that cluster, but with the names of all the victims inscribed on a separate ground-level plaque.

The memorial was designed by the architects *Carmody Groarke*, and was commissioned by the Department of Culture; it was unveiled by the Prince of Wales on the fourth anniversary of the attacks. It has been widely praised, particularly by the relatives of the dead, as a particularly fitting memorial.

Move on again down Park Lane to the south-east corner of the park. You will come to **Achilles** [6], (see illustration, left) a huge bronze by *Richard Westmacott* in 1822. This was the first public monument to the Duke of Wellington, erected (as its plinth states) at the command of George IV. It was made from French cannon captured in the Iron Duke's victories at Vittoria, Salamanca, Toulouse and Waterloo. The title 'Achilles' misleads: *Westmacott's* inspiration was actually the anonymous horse-tamer in the Classical Roman group on Monte Cavallo in Rome, where *Westmacott* spent a formative part of his early career. The extremely modest fig leaf was added after the statue was unveiled to assuage the outraged sensibilities of the Ladies of England, who paid for the statue. The sword followed much later still, in 1862. Statue and plinth stand 11 metres (36 feet) high, and the statue itself remains the largest non-royal commemorative statue in London.

Directly opposite **Achilles**, marooned in the middle of Park Lane itself, in what was Hamilton Gardens but since the widening of Park Lane has become an isolated traffic island, is **Byron [7]**. You should only attempt a close-up inspection if you are quick on your feet as the road is always extremely busy. This statue is an 1880 bronze of George Gordon, Lord Byron – poet, romantic, roué and, ultimately, a hero of the Greek War of Independence – ostensibly by *Richard Belt*, but also allegedly the work of *Pierre Verhyden*, who worked in *Belt's* studio. The controversy involved a two-year libel action brought by *Belt*, who had made the allegation that the statue was really *Verhyden*'s work; *Belt* won this action. The pink granite of the plinth was given by Greece.

The statue's tenuous connection with this location is the nearby site in Piccadilly Terrace (now disappeared) of Byron's extremely short-lived matrimonial home. He married Anne Milbanke in January 1815 and was separated from her in murky and scandalous circumstances barely a year later (by a nice coincidence, his wife's aunt was also the mother-in-law of the celebrated and notorious Lady Caroline Lamb, who had been wildly infatuated with Byron). Byron left England immediately after the separation, never to return, and died at Missolonghi in Greece in 1823. Lady Byron died only in 1860, and Byron's reputation in Victorian England (which was much less exalted than it was abroad) was such that it took the influence of his fellow writer (and then Prime Minister) Benjamin Disraeli to get this statue commissioned.

Exploring the Park and Gardens

Immediately to the south of **Achilles**, at the entrance to South Carriage Drive, is **Queen Elizabeth Gate [8]**, built to commemorate the ninetieth birthday of Queen Elizabeth the Queen Mother. The gate was not inaugurated until 1993, three years after her ninetieth birthday. The commemoration, in the shape of the garish, spun-sugarish, silver-coloured gates by *David Wynne* and *Giuseppe Lund* is more kitsch than royal monument. You will see a more fitting memorial to the Queen Mother on the walk on pages 34–45.

Turn away from Park Lane and walk along the Serpentine Road a short way. Almost immediately on the right, just past the first enclosure and set back from the north side of the road, is the **Cavalry of the Empire Memorial [9]**, by *Adrian Jones* in 1924, and now commemorating the cavalry fallen in both world wars and on active service thereafter. First erected at Stanhope Gate and moved here in 1961, the memorial is a mounted St George standing over a vanquished dragon and bears the

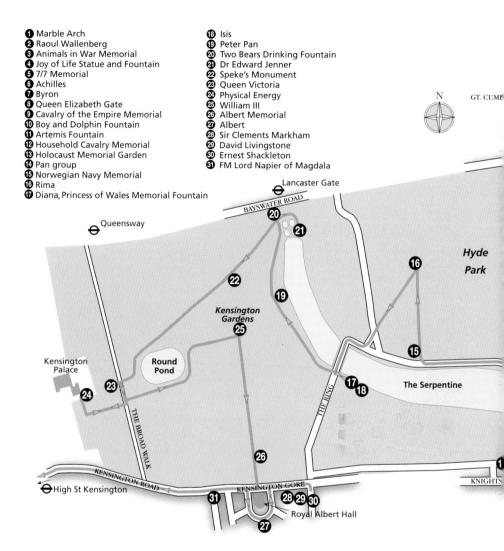

❶ Marble Arch
❷ Raoul Wallenberg
❸ Animals in War Memorial
❹ Joy of Life Statue and Fountain
❺ 7/7 Memorial
❻ Achilles
❼ Byron
❽ Queen Elizabeth Gate
❾ Cavalry of the Empire Memorial
❿ Boy and Dolphin Fountain
⓫ Artemis Fountain
⓬ Household Cavalry Memorial
⓭ Holocaust Memorial Garden
⓮ Pan group
⓯ Norwegian Navy Memorial
⓰ Rima
⓱ Diana, Princess of Wales Memorial Fountain

⓲ Isis
⓳ Peter Pan
⓴ Two Bears Drinking Fountain
㉑ Dr Edward Jenner
㉒ Speke's Monument
㉓ Queen Victoria
㉔ Physical Energy
㉕ William III
㉖ Albert Memorial
㉗ Albert
㉘ Sir Clements Markham
㉙ David Livingstone
㉚ Ernest Shackleton
㉛ FM Lord Napier of Magdala

names of all the cavalry regiments of the British Empire in the Great War. A number of the Indian regiments have names that are historically so evocative – Hodson's Horse, Skinner's Horse and so on – and also are very much alive as units of the modern Indian and Pakistani armies. Most of the British regiments, by contrast, seem to have been amalgamated to the point of extinction.

To the south of the Serpentine Road and opposite the **Cavalry Memorial** lies the park's small area of formal gardens, where there are two more statues. The first is *Alexander Munro's* 1860 **Boy and Dolphin Fountain [10]**, in the middle of the Rose Garden. It is a small marble fountain on a stone plinth. The second is the **Artemis Fountain [11]**, a few yards to the west, an 1899 bronze by *Lady Feodora Gleichen* of a proudly erect but rather flat-chested naked Artemis about to loose her arrow towards Hyde Park Corner. Until her cousin George V's disclaimer of all his German titles in 1917,

Lady Feodora was Her Serene Highness Countess Feodora Gleichen, and for the last 30 years of her life from 1892 she was a regular exhibitor at the Royal Academy. According to the *ODNB*, she 'produced a large number of sculptures which, while not disclosing any great originality, yet are very decidedly above the amateur standard', and she achieved the posthumous honour of becoming the first female member of the Royal Society of British Sculptors.

Leave the rose garden by the gate to the west of **Artemis**, and directly to the south of these two fountains, beside South Carriage Drive, a sombre slate panel lies within a low hedge as the **Household Cavalry Memorial [12]** to the four members of the Blues and Royals (one of the two regiments of the Household Cavalry) killed by an IRA bomb at this spot on 20 July 1982. They were killed as the daily troop made its journey from the Knightsbridge Cavalry Barracks to mount guard at Horse Guards. A little to the west, just into the park from Albert Gate, the drinking trough (previously located on the Victoria Embankment) was presented to the Household Cavalry in 1985 as a memorial to the horses killed and injured by that bomb.

From the drinking trough, proceed away from the South Carriage Drive. Just to the east of The Dell, the small copse below the dam at the east end of the Serpentine, is the **Holocaust Memorial Garden [13]**, which was created in 1983. Designed by *Seifert & Partners* and landscaped by *Derek Lovejoy & Partners*, it features four boulders on gravel, surrounded by silver birch trees, with an English and Hebrew inscription from Lamentations 'For these I weep'.

Return to South Carriage Drive and proceed west to Edinburgh Gate. In front of a new luxury residential development that has replaced the former Bowater House, is a work by *Jacob Epstein*. This piece – a bronze of the god **Pan [14]** urging on a running family group and a dog – is the latest of all *Jacob Epstein*'s works mentioned in this book, having been erected posthumously in 1961.

Retrace your steps, round the east end of the Serpentine and then head along its north side until you see what appears at first sight to be a small meteorite on the grass, some yards back from the water. It is in fact a large lump of rough, unadorned rock. The rock is from Norway and is the **Norwegian Navy Memorial [15]**, a gift in 1948 from the Royal Norwegian Navy and the Norwegian Merchant Fleet in gratitude to the British People for their 'friendship and hospitality during the Second World War'.

Walk up the slope away from the lake to the south side of the Hudson Memorial Bird Sanctuary, just to the west of Ranger's Lodge. William Henry Hudson, ornithologist, naturalist and author, wrote prolifically on nature and particularly birds. Probably his best-known book, his novel *Green Mansions*, had as its heroine **Rima [16]**, a wild and beautiful girl of the woods, and she gives her name to the stone memorial to Hudson at the Bird Sanctuary. By *Jacob Epstein* in 1925, three years after Hudson's death, this is a relief of a female nude with birds, set in a long, stone wall, with water pools in front. At the time it was considered hugely shocking and was even daubed with green paint in protest. Today it seems the very model of reserve and decorum. The design of the memorial was by *Lionel Pearson*, and the lettering by *Eric Gill*.

Cross the Serpentine Bridge and return briefly to the south side of the Serpentine in order to view the **Diana, Princess of Wales Memorial Fountain [17]**. Possibly the most ill-starred monument in London, a hybrid of water feature, playground and impenetrably obscure memorial, it was designed by *Kathryn Gustafson* and was inaugurated by The Queen on 6 July 2004, almost seven years after Diana's death. The fountain was beset by problems very soon after opening – there were problems with it malfunctioning and three people were hospitalized after paddling in the water and slipping. It reopened in August 2004, only to be closed again in December for drainage improvement work to be carried out. It finally reopened in May 2005 and wardens now patrol the site.

Turn westwards from the Memorial Fountain towards the Serpentine Bridge, passing into Kensington Gardens. At the junction of the Serpentine bank and the path which you descended from the roadway, you will see *Simon Gudgeon*'s **Isis [18]**, a three metre (ten feet) high bronze bird, named after the Egyptian Goddess of Nature and inspired by the classical bird, the ibis. **Isis** was commissioned by the Royal Parks Foundation, not least as a fundraising exercise for a new education centre in the Park, the object being to raise £1 million by selling the 1,000 personalized plaques set round the sculpture's base. From **Isis** you continue under the Serpentine Bridge and along the south side of Long Water (as the lake becomes beyond the bridge) to visit an old favourite, **Peter Pan [19]**, one of London's best-loved statues. This bronze by *George Frampton* was the gift in 1912 of Sir James Barrie, the author and creator of the original Peter Pan. The statue was erected secretly behind screens on 29 and 30 April, so as to appear as if by magic on the 1 May.

At the top of Long Water are the Italian Gardens, which were built in 1861 to provide filter beds for the Serpentine. They are the only example in a London park of this sort of formal garden, which – as their name suggests – would be more at home in Italy, or France, and are made the more conspicuous by the informality of the rest of Kensington Gardens. At the north-west corner of the gardens, close to Marlborough Gate, is one of the smallest works that you will see on any of the walks in this book, the **Two Bears Drinking Fountain [20]**. This bronze fountain, surmounted by two small embracing bears, was presented in 1939 by the Metropolitan Drinking Fountain and Cattle Trough Association to mark its eightieth anniversary. It is a small reminder of the association's role in London before the advent of the internal combustion engine. The association provided the essential drinking troughs, the petrol stations of their day, which can still be seen on some London streets.

On the east side of the Italian Gardens is a rather more substantial bronze of **Dr Edward Jenner [21]** by *William Calder Marshall* in 1858. Jenner, who died in 1823, had first discovered immunization against smallpox as early as 1796, an astonishingly early date when you think that the World Health Organization only declared smallpox finally eradicated as recently as 1980. His statue was first erected in Trafalgar Square, not least because the Prince Consort was *Calder Marshall's* principal patron. The Office of Works, however, which was the government body responsible for public statues in the Victorian age, had always been opposed to placing **Jenner** in Trafalgar Square. It wanted to reserve the square for soldiers and statesmen, so after Prince Albert's death in 1861 **Jenner** was removed. When it was re-erected in 1862 in its present site, it was Kensington Gardens' first public statue.

Moving on in a south-westerly direction, towards Kensington Palace, you come to **Speke's Monument [22]**. The 1866 obelisk's architect was *Philip Hardwick*. Engraved with the simple legend 'In memory of Speke – Victoria Nyanza and the Nile 1864', it is the monument to the great Victorian

explorer John Hanning Speke, who died in that year. Speke's greatest triumphs were his discovery of Lake Victoria with Richard Francis Burton in 1858 and his confirmation of its north outlet as the source of the Nile in 1862.

From the junction close to **Speke's Monument**, continue to head down one of the principal avenues leading to the Round Pond, to the first of the four statues of **Queen Victoria [23]** described in the walks in this book. This statue is on the east side of Kensington Palace and looks out over the Round Pond towards **'Physical Energy' [24]** (see illustration, above) in the distance. It is a marble, and is now rather badly worn by the elements. It was erected in 1893 at the instigation (and expense) of the citizens of Kensington to mark, rather belatedly, the Golden Jubilee of Queen Victoria (which was in 1887), who was born in the palace and lived there until her accession in 1837. Its most interesting feature is the identity of its sculptress, who was Queen Victoria's daughter, *HRH Princess Louise*. The Princess is also diversely commemorated by Lake Louise in Alberta (her husband, the Duke of Argyll, was governor-general of Canada) and by a pub in Holborn.

On the south side of the palace, just inside the fine late-seventeenth century iron gates, is one of two statues of **William III [25]** in central London. This is a rather severe depiction, but also a flamboyant one, with the King appearing almost as a wickedly debonair Carolean Cavalier. It betrays, perhaps, its Germanic authorship: its sculptor was *Heinrich Baucke*, it was cast in Berlin and it was the gift of Kaiser Wilhelm II to Edward VII 'for the British Nation' in 1907. Behind **William III**, on the parapet of the palace, the four large urns, each from a single block of Portland stone, are the work of *Caius Gabriel Cibber*, whose more famous contribution to London's public statuary you will see on the walk on pages 54–63.

From the moment you left the **Diana Princess of Wales Memorial Fountain** you will have had distant glimpses from east, north and now west of a large equestrian sculpture in the middle of the gardens. As you look east from the palace over the Round Pond, the sculpture is clearly framed in the gap in the trees on the slight ridge in the middle of the gardens, before the ground falls gently away to Long Water below. Possibly the most striking bronze in both park and gardens, if not also the best-located public sculpture in London, this is **'Physical Energy'** [25] (see illustration, page 21) by *G. F. Watts*, one of the greatest Victorian artists, although a sculptor only relatively late on in his career. In itself this is an extraordinary depiction, or embodiment, of energy, with the straining sinews and muscles of horse and rider. The bronze is made all the more conspicuous by its location at the crossing point of several of the gardens' principal avenues: to the west, the Round Pond and the Palace, and to the south, down the avenue of trees, the Albert Memorial, which you will see very shortly. **'Physical Energy'** had an elephantine gestation, for *Watts* first began working on the concept in the 1870s. In 1902, when *Watts* accepted his only public honour by becoming one of the original twelve founding members of the Order of Merit (having twice declined Gladstone's earlier offers of a baronetcy), he also consented to the suggestion that a cast of 'Physical Energy' should be incorporated in the memorial to Cecil Rhodes at Groote Schuur in South Africa. It is a second cast that you see today in Kensington Gardens, but the original sculpture itself can also be seen at the Watts Gallery outside Guildford. You will come across another *Watts*' piece on the walk on pages 100–9, in the very different circumstances of Postman's Park in the City.

Commemorating Prince Albert

And so to Prince Albert, who is conspicuously commemorated in this corner of London. The architect of the **Albert Memorial [26]** (see illustration, right) was *George Gilbert Scott* (who is not to be confused with his grandson, *Giles*, whose work you will see on other walks in this book), and the principal sculptor – of Albert himself – was *John Foley* (Queen Victoria's preference, *Carlo Marochetti*, having died in 1867 during the design of the memorial and without having accepted the commission). In fact the work was finished after *Foley's* own death by *Thomas Brock*. The memorial was unveiled in 1872, the central statue of Albert three years later. *Scott* regarded the memorial as his 'most prominent work' and the outcome of his 'highest and most enthusiastic efforts'.

It is 53 metres (174 feet) high and comprises more than 175 life-size or larger figures. Around the canopy immediately above the four arches is the inscription 'Queen Victoria and her people / to the memory of Albert Prince Consort / as a tribute of their gratitude / for a life devoted to the public good'. At the four corners of the canopy are stone groups representing Engineering (NW) by *John Lawlor*, Commerce (NE) by *Thomas Thornycroft*, Manufacturing (SE) by *Henry Weekes* and Agriculture (SW) by *William Calder Marshall*. At the corresponding outer corners of the whole memorial are further stone groups representing America by *John Bell*, Africa by *W. Theed*, Asia by *Foley* and Europe by *Patrick Macdowell*. Other sculptors were *J. B. Philip* and *H. H. Armstead*. Around the central area are eight figures symbolizing the natural sciences; in the niches of the spire are Faith, Hope, Charity and Humility; and at the angles Prudence, Temperance, Justice and Fortitude. Seated in the middle of this praise, tribute and commemoration, from an adoring widowed queen whose grief knew no bounds, is Albert himself.

A hundred years after its first unveiling, the whole memorial was in such bad disrepair that Londoners had almost become used to its being permanently shrouded in scaffolding and

sheeting. But in the 1990s English Heritage spent over £11 million on the restoration of the memorial to its pristine original splendour. It was unveiled by The Queen in 1998.

The memorial faces Albert's even more conspicuous monument, the Albert Hall, designed by *Francis Fowke* and (after his death in mid-project) *H. Y. D. Scott*, and opened in 1871. Skirt around the building (unless your walk coincides with a concert that you want to hear) and make your way to the other statue of **Albert [27]** on the south side of the hall. In his lifetime, Albert had been anxious to avoid a statue commemorating his leading role in the staging of the Great Exhibition of 1851, and the commemorative commission won by *Joseph Durham* had been to provide a statue of Britannia. After Albert's death in December 1861, however, Queen Victoria was anxious to commission a statue of him without delay and so *Durham* produced this instead. It was initially erected in 1863 in the then Royal Horticultural Gardens, which lay between today's Prince Consort Road and Imperial College Road and were held by the Royal Horticultural Society (RHS) under a lease from the Commissioners of the Great Exhibition. When the gardens became too expensive for the RHS to maintain and were closed in 1882, **Albert** was moved to his present location in front of the by then completed hall.

Between Queens Gate and Alexandra Gate

After the magnificence of Albert's monuments, this walk ends with two brief diversions to four smaller works, all on the south side of Kensington Gore between Queens Gate and Alexandra Gate, three to the east of the Albert Hall and the fourth to the west. By the main entrance of the Royal Geographical Society (RGS) at the corner of Exhibition Road is a small bronze bust of a former President of the society, **Sir Clements Markham [28]**, by *F. W. Pomeroy* in 1921, a gift of the Peruvian nation for historical services rendered. On the Kensington Gore frontage of the RGS is a bronze statue of **David Livingstone [29]**, perhaps the most famous of all the Victorian explorers, not least thanks to Henry Stanley and his famous greeting, 'Dr Livingstone, I presume?' Stanley was himself a distinguished explorer as well as a journalist, administrator, author and Member of Parliament, besides also being a veteran of both sides of the American Civil War; this was by *T. B. Huxley-Jones* in 1953.

On the Exhibition Road frontage is **Ernest Shackleton [30]**, by *Charles Jagger* in 1932. Shackleton is one of the great names in British Antarctic exploration and is probably best known for leading the *Endurance* expedition of 1914–16. Early in 1915 the *Endurance* became trapped in ice and sank ten months later. In April 1916 Shackleton and the crew sailed to Elephant Island, and then Shackleton and five other crew set off to find help. They travelled across 1,126 km (700 miles) of the Southern Ocean to South Georgia. Not one member of the expedition died. It was one of the greatest feats of heroic maritime endeavour of the early twentieth century.

Finally, at the top of Queensgate stands *Edgar Boehm's* 1891 bronze of **Field Marshal Lord Napier of Magdala [31]**. First erected in Waterloo Place in 1892, the year after Napier's death, the statue was moved in 1921 to make room for the present statue of Edward VII. Napier was one of the small band of distinguished Victorian generals who specialized in fighting (and winning) brief and efficient Imperial wars, Napier himself taking his title from his capture of Magdala in conclusion of his Abyssinian campaign of 1868 (when the same Henry Stanley mentioned above was the principal 'embedded' journalist accompanying Napier). The plinth bears the ineffably superior legend 'He rests in St Paul's Cathedral'.

Walk west along Kensington Road, which runs into Kensington High Street and the Underground station is on your left-hand side.

2. BELGRAVIA – FROM VICTORIA STATION TO HYDE PARK CORNER

START	Victoria Station (Victoria, Circle and District Underground lines; overground and bus/coach services)
FINISH	Hyde Park Corner Underground Station (Piccadilly line)
DISTANCE	2 km (1 ¼ miles)
DURATION	45 minutes

This walk begins at Victoria Station, which is one of London's half-dozen great railway termini. In origin, it is in fact two separate and more or less contemporaneous stations of 1860, the western one built by the London Brighton and South Coast Railway, and the eastern by the London Chatham and Dover, both with later Edwardian facades fronting the bus station on the forecourt. The Grosvenor Hotel on Buckingham Palace Road, built in part over the London and Brighton station, is High Victorian Gothic. It is rivalled only by its near contemporaries, the Langham Hotel (see page 66) and the Midland Grand Hotel at St Pancras, which is now in the course of restoration in order to supplement the Eurostar train service from St Pancras Station (see pages 118–19).

Three Curios

Take the Wilton Road exit from the tube, and turn right out of the exit, proceeding to the traffic lights. Three little curios are visible from this spot. On the island at the junction is **Little Ben [1]**, a 9-metre (29 ½-foot) high cast-iron clock tower of 1892 by *Gillett & Johnston*, bearing very little resemblance to its supposed senior sibling at the other end of Victoria Street. It was removed in 1964, but replaced by Westminster City Council in 1981 with the help of Elf Aquitaine, 'offered as a gesture of Franco-British friendship'. A plaque records Little Ben's Apology for Summer Time: 'My hands you may retard or may advance – My heart beats true for England as for France'.

On the other side of Victoria Street stands the **Victoria Palace Theatre [2]**, of 1911, whose architect *Frank Matcham* was also responsible for the earlier Coliseum in St Martin's Lane, and for the Opera House in Buxton. On the cupola above the theatre is a delightful gilded ballerina, by an unknown hand, and below her are two semi-clad stone Muses; the one to the left appears to be either pointing at the ballerina or hailing a taxi.

To the left of the theatre is Allington Street, and at its junction with Victoria Street is **Saga House [3]**, a bland and generally undistinguished 1997 office block. Over its corner entrance, however, is a bizarrely sculpted porch by *Barry Baldwin*, with three-quarter relief images of rather aggressive beasts of the ocean and jungle – a shark, a tiger, an elephant with particularly rampant tusks and trunk, various birds and over the middle of the entrance a baboon whose depiction pulls no punches.

Grosvenor Gardens

You are going to move on to more serious statuary. Retrace your steps up Wilton Road to the traffic lights, and cross the road to Lower Grosvenor Gardens. On the south side of the Gardens, with his head almost lost in most unmilitary fashion in the branches of the plane trees, stands a mounted **Maréchal Ferdinand Foch [4]** (see illustration, right), supreme commander of the Allied Armies in France in 1918. This is a bronze by *Georges Malissard*. Another cast stands in Cassel in Flanders, where Foch had his headquarters as an army commander at the beginning of the Great War. Foch was accorded remarkably high honours by the English. Besides being one of the only two French military leaders with a statue in central London (for the other one see page 139), he was also awarded a field marshal's baton, the Order of Merit, a knighthood in the Order of the Bath and a Doctorate of Civil Law. The right flank of his pedestal bears the legend 'I am conscious of having served England as I served my own country'. It was nicely appropriate, and perhaps not entirely coincidental, that on the same day as **Foch** was unveiled by the Prince of Wales – 5 June 1930 – the then Marquis de Montcalm was unveiling the statue at Greenwich of his ancestor's adversary, **General James Wolfe** (see page 140).

The two little rectangular lodges, with their shell and pebbledash exteriors and pediments on all four sides, which are the only other structures in Lower Grosvenor Gardens, were the gift of the French government in 1952, being designed by *M. Moreux*, the architect-in-chief of French national monuments and palaces.

Immediately to the north are Upper Grosvenor Gardens. In the middle of their triangle is *Jonathan Kenworthy's* 1998 bronze of **Lioness and Lesser Kudu [5]**, a one and a half times life-size pair commissioned by the Duke of Westminster 'to mark the opening of Upper Grosvenor Gardens to the people of Westminster' and unveiled in June 2000. At the top corner of the gardens, at the junction of Hobart Place and Grosvenor Gardens, is *John Tweed's* 1925 **Rifle Brigade Memorial [6]**. Its centrepiece is a raised life-size bronze of a rifleman of the Great War; below him are two light infantry soldiers of the Napoleonic Wars; to his right, a rifleman of 1806 and to his left an officer of 1800. As with so many memorials to the two world wars, it is the words, or rather the numbers, of the inscriptions that are the most moving elements of an exceptionally fine sculpted memorial. The original memorial honours the 11,575 officers, warrant officers, non-commissioned officers and riflemen of The Rifle Brigade who fell in the Great War. The subsequent lower plaque commemorates the staggering greater number of 13,290 members of the Corps of The Rifle Brigade who fell in the Second World War.

Belgrave Square

Leave the gardens and turn left into Hobart Place. Walk down the road past 'the tiny No 5 Hobart Place, *c*.1870, which conjures ridiculously with the Grosvenor Gardens style', as Pevsner so nicely puts it, and then turn right and walk up Upper Belgrave Street to the eastern corner of Belgrave Square. Cross the road so that you are on the pavement around the perimeter of the central gardens. This is the centre of Belgravia, at the heart of the Grosvenor Estate's domain, and it was the village of Belgrave on the Grosvenor estates in Cheshire that gave both square and area their names. The development of Belgravia and Pimlico was principally the achievement of Robert Grosvenor, 1st Marquess of Westminster, a bronze of whom you will see shortly. The square was laid out in twenty or so years from 1812, the two principal architects being *James Wyatt* and *George Basevi*, with the great Victorian developer Thomas Cubitt as the principal builder.

FOCH
1851 - 1929

Notwithstanding that very English background – tempered today, it must be admitted, by the fact that the square contains the greatest concentration of foreign embassies in London – Belgrave Square has managed in the last few years to become the principal London home to Latin, or Iberian, American memorials. In the corner where you are standing is *Hugo Daini's* 1974 bronze of **Simon Bolivar [7]**, 'Liberator of Venezuela Colombia Ecuador Peru and Panama and Founder of Bolivia'. He stands in a declamatory pose, and it is not hard to imagine that he is uttering the words attributed to him in the inscription on the right flank of his pedestal: 'I am convinced that England alone is capable of protecting the world's precious rights as she is great glorious and wise'. This statue of the pre-eminent hero of the early nineteenth-century liberation of the South American republics was erected on behalf of those countries, and was unveiled by James Callaghan, the then Foreign Secretary.

Before you walk clockwise around the square, take a brief detour for a few yards in the opposite direction along the north-east frontage of the gardens. This will enable you to look into the gardens and see **Homage to Leonardo [8]**, begun by *Enzo Plazzotta* and completed in 1982, after his death, by *Mark Holloway*. It is a bronze realization of Leonardo da Vinci's Vitruvian Man, a torso with two pairs of legs and arms, surrounded by both a square and a circle, demonstrating that the span of a man's outspread arms is equal to his height.

Now walk in a clockwise direction around the square, past **Bolivar**, to the southern corner where you will find **Christopher Columbus [9]** (see illustration, right)– or if you prefer, because the inscription on the plinth is in English and Spanish, **Cristóbal Colón**. This is a 1992 bronze by *Tomas Bañuelos,* the 'generous gift of the Spanish people to all the peoples of the Americas' to commemorate the five hundredth anniversary 'of the encounter of the two worlds', for (in the words of the doggerel) it was 'in fourteen hundred and ninety-two Columbus sailed the ocean blue'. Notwithstanding his un-maritime origins as the son of a Genoese woolcomber, Columbus's discovery of the New World – probably Watling's Island in the Bahamas, on Friday 12 October 1492 – makes him, half a millennium later, by far the most famous of all the great explorers.

Cross the road, in the direction of Belgrave Place, to the end building in the southern terrace, now the **Norwegian Embassy [10]**. On either side of the main entrance on the Belgrave Place flank are two Coade-stone (an eighteenth-century composite and reconstituted material) relief panels, dating from 1796, when they were originally installed at the Danish–Norwegian Consulate in Wellclose Square in Stepney. They were re-erected here in 1968. Both panels show allegorical cherubs, with 'arts' to the left and 'agriculture' to the right. You will see another rather larger example of Coade stone in the guise of the **South Bank Lion** if you do the walk on pages 73–81.

Cross back over the road to the perimeter of the gardens and proceed along the south-west side. Just a few yards inside the garden's locked gates you will see a bust of **George Basevi [11]**, the architect responsible for the majority of the buildings in the square, apart from the four corner houses. This is a 2000 bronze by *Jonathan Wylder* (whose gallery is in Motcomb Street just off the west corner of the square). Basevi was a fine classical architect – witness his buildings here – whose best-known commission is the Fitzwilliam Museum in Cambridge. He was also the uncle of Benjamin Disraeli, Earl of Beaconsfield, his sister Maria having been Disraeli's mother. Basevi was killed at the age of fifty-one in 1845 when he fell in the course of an inspection of the bell tower of Ely Cathedral.

At the west corner of the gardens is *Simoes de Almeida's* 2002 bronze of **Prince Henry the Navigator [12]**, who perhaps has a marginally better claim than the tenants of the other three corners to a statue in a London square since, although his father was John I, King of Portugal, his mother was Philippa, daughter of John of Gaunt, who was himself a son of Edward III and a colossus of fourteenth-century English politics. Henry (1394–1460) founded an observatory and school of scientific navigation at Cape St Vincent (he was also Governor of the Algarve), and the inscription on the plaque in the paving stone before his statue deserves to be quoted in full: 'His study of late mediaeval travellers' reports together with his knowledge of cartography and cosmology led him to reject the traditional belief in the inaccessibility of the oceans south of the Canary Islands. It was [his] vision that enabled the whole Atlantic coastline of Africa, the eventual route to India, to be opened up to navigation and trade'. The statue was officially inaugurated by the President of Portugal in February 2002.

Continue round to the north corner and you will find **General Don José de San Martin [13]** (1778 – 1850). 'Founder of the Argentine Independence, he also gave freedom to Chile and Peru' proclaims the front of his plinth. On its right flank 'His name represents democracy justice and liberty' and on the left flank 'The Argentine British community in Argentina to the People of London'. It is a bronze by *Juan Carlos Ferraro* of 1993, cast in Buenos Aires, and unveiled by the Duke of Edinburgh in 1994.

CHRISTOPHER
COLUMBUS

Between the Square and the Corner

Opposite **San Martin**, on the island at the junction of Wilton and Grosvenor Crescents, stands the developer of Belgrave Square, **Sir Robert Grosvenor KG, 1st Marquess of Westminster [14]** (1767–1845). It is a 1998 bronze by *Jonathan Wylder* and commissioned by the present Duke of Westminster. **Sir Robert** stands, leaning forwards, an architect's plan in his hands and two Talbot hounds at his feet (Talbots were added to the Grosvenor arms in the seventeenth century). The milestone also at his feet records the distance of 197 miles to Chester, and the Grosvenor estates in Cheshire, although the story of the Grosvenor family's great landed wealth really began two centuries earlier when, in the seventeeth century, Sir Thomas Grosvenor, the 3rd baronet, prudently married one Mary Davies, whose dowry included part of the Manor of Ebury – today's Mayfair and Belgravia.

Cross the road into Wilton Crescent and follow the road round and up into Wilton Place. Walk until you see St Paul's Church on your right-hand side. You have only come to see a small plaque rather than a more substantial sculpture, but it is a no less moving memorial for that, for it commemorates the bravest of women. The plaque is on the exterior of the north wall of the church commemorating the dead of the **Women's Transport Service (FANY) [15]** of 1939–45. The First Aid Nursing Yeomanry was formed in 1907 and still exists a century later, although it is now known as The Princess Royal's Volunteer Corps, or FANY (PRVC). Its diversification from its nursing origins led to many of the female agents in the British Special Operations Executive (SOE) during

1. Little Ben
2. Victoria Palace Theatre
3. Saga House
4. Maréchal Ferdinand Foch
5. Lioness and Lesser Kudu
6. Rifle Brigade Memorial
7. Simon Bolivar
8. Homage to Leonardo
9. Christopher Columbus
10. Norwegian Embassy
11. George Basevi
12. Prince Henry the Navigator
13. General Don José de San Martin
14. Sir Robert Grosvenor
15. Women's Transport Service (FANY)
16. Hyde Park Screen
17. Wellington Arch
18. Peace Descending on Quadriga of War
19. Duke of Wellington
20. Machine Gun Corps Memorial
21. Australian War Memorial
22. New Zealand Memorial
23. Royal Artillery Monument
24. Memorial Gates

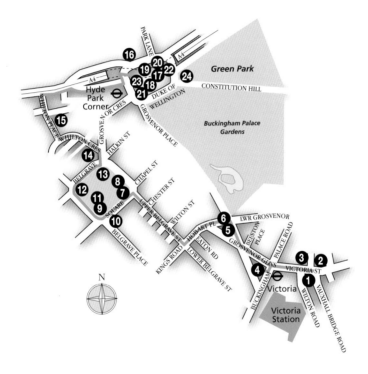

the Second World War being commissioned into the corps. The fifty-two names commemorated by the memorial hold, between them, two George Crosses (GC, which ranks equal with the Victoria Cross as Britain's highest award for valour) and six French Croix de Guerre. Among the dead are twelve who died in concentration camps, including Violette Szabo GC, who was executed in Ravensbruck in February 1945. Below the main memorial is a separate plaque commemorating another famous SOE 'FANY', Odette Hallowes GC, who survived the war by half a century.

Hyde Park Corner

Continue up Wilton Place, turn right into Knightsbridge and then walk east to Hyde Park Corner, where the huge island site contains one of the densest concentrations of statues and memorials in London. The safest place to cross over is at the traffic lights in the top left corner, by the **Hyde**

Park Screen [16] immediately to the west of Apsley House. This house is the historic home of the Dukes of Wellington and has the grandest of postal addresses, 'Number One, London'.

Walk across to the middle of the island site and take a closer look at *Decimus Burton's* 1825 **Wellington Arch [17]**. Once again, this too has been moved since it was first built in 1826–8. The arch originally stood at the top left-hand (north-west) corner of the present island, opposite the screen (also by *Burton*, of the same period, with its sculpted friezes by *Hening*, father *John* and brothers *John Jnr* and *Samuel*). It was originally intended as a ceremonial entrance to Buckingham Palace and Green Park, but was never completed as *Burton* intended. The arch was translated into another monument to Wellington, and in 1846 a colossal 9-metre (30-foot) tall equestrian statue of the Duke by *Matthew Cotes Wyatt* was placed on top of it. In 1885, Hyde Park Corner having become Victorian London's worst traffic bottleneck, the arch was dismantled and re-erected on its present alignment with Constitution Hill, and the Duke's statue was taken to Aldershot, where it still remains.

Today's **Peace Descending on the Quadriga of War [18]** was commissioned in 1907 from *Adrian Jones* (whose background as an army veterinary surgeon must have assisted his mastery of equine sculpture). Its 38-ton bulk was placed on top of the arch in 1912, a gift to the nation by Lord Michelham of Hellingly. The arch repays a modest climb to its parapet, from where you can survey The Queen's gardens behind Buckingham Palace and the view down Constitution Hill to Westminster.

On the north side of the island, immediately opposite the front of Apsley House, is the 1888 smaller replacement statue of the **Duke of Wellington [19]**, by *Edgar Boehm*. This is a bronze of the mounted Duke, with four bronze foot soldiers at the corners of the red granite pedestal representing The Black Watch, the Royal Welsh Fusiliers, the Inniskilling Dragoons and the 1st Foot Guards.

To the east of the **Duke**, opposite the bottom of Park Lane, is the **Machine Gun Corps Memorial [20]** (see illustration, page 33). It is a naked Hermes by *Francis Derwent Wood* in 1925, with wreathed machine guns and the chilling text from I Samuel 18:7, 'Saul hath slain in his thousands, but David in his tens of thousands'. You can see a near copy of this Boy David by *Edward Bainbridge Copnall* on Chelsea Embankment (see page 127).

In the south-west quadrant of the island is the second most recent of Hyde Park Corner's memorials, the **Australian War Memorial [21]**, designed by the firm of *Tonkin Zulaikha Greer* and unveiled by The Queen on Armistice Day 2003. Its interlocking grey marble slabs are engraved with the names of Australian forces' battle sites and the place names of origin of Australian servicemen. It also bears the eloquently brief lines of Robert Menzies, Australia's Prime Minister in 1941, 'Whatever burden you are to carry / We will also shoulder that burden'.

The newest monument on the island, in its north-east corner, is the **New Zealand Memorial [22]** (the word 'war' was deliberately omitted from the title), whose architect and sculptor were *John Hardwick-Smith* and *Paul Dibble*. It was unveiled – again by The Queen – on Armistice Day 2006. This rather strange memorial, comprising sixteen black metal girders embedded in the ground and all angled slightly to the south, is engraved with aspects of New Zealand's cultural, sporting, military and agricultural life. It '...commemorates the enduring bonds between New Zealand and the United Kingdom and our shared sacrifice during times of war. It is a symbol both of our common heritage and of New Zealand's distinct national identity...'; the text is then repeated in Maori. If you can see in it soldiers in procession, Maori ancestral sites or Celtic remains, and if the forward-leaning angle of the girders suggests a defiant pose reminiscent of warriors doing the *haka*, the defensive bat in cricket and the barrel of a shouldered gun, you are perceptively understanding the professed intentions of the memorial's creators.

The memorial expresses impeccable sentiments and commemorates Britain's ties with its furthest, but in many ways also closest, former dominion. Australia is already commemorated here, why not New Zealand too? Yet Hyde Park Corner, with the work of *Jagger* and *Burton, Jones* and *Boehm* already on a fairly cluttered small island site, seems a mistake for this very much more stark and brutal work. It might have been better to follow the example of the **Canadian War Memorial** (see page 36), with its own solitary site in the largely untapped open spaces of Green Park.

On the west side of the island, opposite the former St George's Hospital and now the Lanesborough Hotel, is perhaps the most powerful and moving of all London's war memorials, the **Royal Artillery Monument [23]** by *Charles Jagger*, with its pedestal and podium by the architect *Lionel Pearson*. Indeed, it is widely recognized as one of the great works of twentieth-century British sculpture. The monument commemorates the 49,076 Royal Artillery men who died in the Great War and the 29,924 who died in the Second World War. The memorial was the product of a remarkably long gestation. The Royal Artillery War Commemoration Fund's memorial sub-committee was formed in early 1919 but the memorial was not unveiled until October 1925.

Schemes were proposed by *Adrian Jones* and *Aston Webb*, and inevitably also by *Baker* and *Lutyens*, the last of whom was the front runner by the end of 1920. But *Lutyens'* scheme was deemed too tall for the Hyde Park Corner site, and besides his sculptor, *Francis Derwent Wood*, had already been commissioned to produce the **Machine Gun Corps Memorial** (see above). An alternative, more horizontal scheme was submitted by *Pearson*, and it was the *Pearson/Jagger* scheme that was eventually accepted in 1922. Two subsequent major changes were made. At a late stage, in 1924, the howitzer was reversed, so as to face downhill and south, towards the Somme, rather than uphill to Hyde Park. At some quite advanced stage, *Jagger* introduced the – at the time deeply shocking – dead artilleryman lying on the ground at the north end, covered by his cape. On the low plinth below him are inscribed the words: 'Here was a royal fellowship of death', the text being taken by *Jagger* from Shakespeare's *Henry V*. It is a remarkable and moving memorial.

This walk's final monument is in the south-east corner of the island, at the top of Constitution Hill. The 2002 **Memorial Gates [24]**, designed by *Liam O'Connor*, are 'In memory of the five million volunteers from the Indian sub-continent, Africa and the Caribbean who fought with Britain in the two world wars'. Two austere piers on either side of the roadway form the main part of the monument, the effect of that austerity being a little marred, however, by the rather exotically Indian pavilion next to the north pier.

Proceed to Hyde Park Underground Station, which lies under the north-west corner of the Hyde Park Corner site. The station can be accessed from various points within Hyde Park Corner's extensive pedestrian underpass system.

3. ST JAMES'S PARK – FROM QUEEN ANNE'S GATE TO KING CHARLES STREET

START	St James's Park Underground Station (Circle and District lines)
FINISH	Westminster Underground Station (Circle, District and Jubilee lines)
DISTANCE	4.25 km (2.6 miles)
DURATION	1 ¼ hours

This walk literally begins at St James's Park Underground Station. You will be looking at sculptures before you've put your ticket away.

55 Broadway

Leave the tube by the Broadway exit at the east end of the platform. St James's is not just another Underground station, for above it are the headquarters of Transport for London at 55 Broadway. Unlike most large office buildings in London it does not have a name. Built in 1929 in the heyday of the London Underground system's excellence between the world wars, the construction of 55 Broadway was under the distinguished management of the remarkable Frank Pick. When it was built it was the tallest office building in London – an extraordinary notion when you look at the City and Canary Wharf only seventy-five years later. The architect of its unusual cruciform shape was *Charles Holden*, who was also responsible for a number of the more distinguished station buildings at the outer ends of the Piccadilly line, besides the layout of Piccadilly Underground Station itself, one of the major hubs of the Underground.

Holden, with the strong support of Pick, insisted on the incorporation of the bold – even, at the time, shocking – sculpture that still today adorns the austere Portland stone exterior of 55 Broadway. In the middle of the south-east and north-east facades, at first-floor level, are **Day** and **Night [1]**, both by *Jacob Epstein*, each comprising a larger and a smaller figure: **Day's** unabashed phallus caused as much outrage as *Epstein's* **Ages of Man** on **Zimbabwe House** (see page 60). As a sort of sporadic frieze round the building, 24 metres (79 feet) up from street level, there are eight horizontal reliefs representing **The Winds [2]**, each wind being depicted twice, on either side of the wing of the cruciform opposite the compass point of that wind. *Eric Gill*, who took overall charge of the reliefs, carved the figures on the east sides of the north and south wings, and the north side of the west wing, while the other five reliefs (clockwise from north) were by *Henry Moore, F. Rabinovitch, Alfred Gerrard, Allan Wyon* and *Eric Aumonier*.

Unfortunately the two figures in the north-west quadrant, by *Gill* and *Aumonier*, can no longer be seen from the street, but the others are worthy examples of the value of John Betjeman's exhortation to 'look above the shopfronts'.

A Brief Diversion

Before you go into the park, make a brief diversion and walk south down Broadway to Christ Church Gardens on the corner of Broadway and Victoria Street, opposite New Scotland Yard, the headquarters of the Metropolitan Police. The garden itself is all that now remains of the Victorian church of the same name that was substantially destroyed by German bombing on 17 April 1941. In the north-west corner is *Edwin Russell's* 1970 flowing bronze scroll, known as the **Suffragette Memorial [3]** and erected by the Suffragette Fellowship. It stands here because as the scroll itself records 'nearby Caxton Hall was historically associated with women's suffrage meetings and deputations to Parliament'. In the opposite corner is **Henry Purcell [4]**, unveiled by Princess Margaret on 22 November 1995, the tercentenary of his death. It is a strange bronze of a large figurative head, surmounted by a wig of floribunda, and entitled by its sculptor *Glynn Williams* 'The flowering of the English Baroque – a memorial to Henry Purcell'. A house on nearby Old Pye Street is said to be the birthplace of Purcell, one of the earliest of the great English composers. One of the main reasons for this diversion is that Purcell is the only composer apart from Sir Arthur Sullivan (see page 78) that you will encounter on the walks in this book.

In the Direction of the Park

Retrace your steps back to St James's Park Underground station, cross the road into Queen Anne's Gate and walk in the direction of St James's Park. The wider, western end of Queen Anne's Gate, formerly Queen Square, used to be separated by a wall and railings from the eastern end, formerly Park Street, until the two ends were united in the 1870s. The former Queen Square end contains a number of surviving pre-Georgian (literally, Queen Anne) houses with spectacularly stunning exteriors. Against the wall of Number 15 on the south side is a marble statue of **Queen Anne [5]**. It dates from 1705 and has been attributed, uncertainly, to *Francis Bird*, who was also responsible for the original of the other statue of Queen Anne that you can see on the walk on pages 82–90. The statue was moved to its present position *c*.1810. Unlike a number of other central London statues that were moved to greater safety during the Second World War, this one was left in situ, but spent the war hidden behind a protective brick wall.

Turn left into Birdcage Walk and walk past the Guards' Chapel, a stark modernist building from the early 1960s. This building replaced the previous chapel that was destroyed with tragic loss of life by a V1 flying bomb during a Sunday-morning service in 1944. Outside the west end of the Chapel stands *James Butler's* 1985 bronze of **Field Marshal Earl Alexander of Tunis [6]**, a Supreme Commander during the Second World War and after the war Governor-General of Canada (1946–1952). Materially larger than life-size, this is a very successful informal pose of 'Alex', which captures very well a likeness seen in many contemporary photographs.

Victoria Memorial

Continue down Birdcage Walk, past the Wellington Barracks, and then turn right into Spur Road, following the perimeter of the park round to the front of Buckingham Palace. You will come to the **Victoria Memorial [7]** (see illustration, right), perhaps the next largest individual memorial in central London after the **Albert Memorial** and, like the **Albert Memorial**, abundant in allegory. This is the masterpiece designed by *Aston Webb* and sculpted by *Thomas Brock*, who was spontaneously knighted by his grateful sovereign, George V, at the unveiling in 1911. The memorial consists of 2,300 tons of marble, 800 tons of granite and 70 tons of bronze feature, and at the centre a seated Victoria gazing down The Mall. Around her, four bronze lions at the base symbolize Power; four other bronze figures represent Peace, Progress, Manufacture and Agriculture; around the marble base cascades, triton, mermaid and a ship's prow symbolize Sea Power. At the same level as the Queen herself are Truth, Justice and Motherhood, while above her are gilded figures representing Courage, Constancy and winged Victory.

Along and Off The Mall

For many years the **Victoria Memorial** was an island in the middle of the *rond-point*, but in recent years it has been reconnected to the palace by the pedestrianization of the roadway between palace and memorial. Cross to the north side of the *rond-point* and pass through Canada Gate, with its opulent decoration by *Alfred Drury*, into the bottom right-hand corner of Green Park, where you will find a rather different memorial. This is the **Canadian War Memorial [8]**, the work of *Pierre Granche* in 1994. Two tilting, pink granite-faced slabs, with bronze maple leaves set into them and a constant wash of water, barely rise out of the ground at all, yet in its different and very much smaller way it is as unusually effective a monument as the peerless Canadian memorial on Vimy Ridge in Flanders.

Return to The Mall and walk along the north side away from Buckingham Palace. About a third of the way along The Mall turn left into Marlborough Road. Walk up the road and on your right, opposite the eastern forecourt of St James's Palace, is Marlborough House. On the outside wall of the garden is *Alfred Gilbert's* 1932 bronze **Queen Alexandra Memorial [9]**. The memorial is here because Marlborough House was the home of Alexandra, Edward VII's consort, in her widowhood, until her own death in 1925. It is a most unusual work for its time and must have looked dated even when new. The bronze flows downwards from the central virtuous Queen like liquid; before her are, as the base is inscribed, 'Faith Hope and Love [her] Guiding Virtues'. Like Brock after the unveiling of Alexandra's mother-in-law Victoria, *Gilbert* was knighted by George V after this unveiling. *Gilbert* had also been the sculptor, thirty years earlier, of perhaps London's most famous single statue, **Eros** (see page 56).

Retrace your steps to the junction of Marlborough Road and The Mall, and immediately round the corner to the left is a small profile relief commemorating **Queen Mary [10]**, George V's consort – a work by *William Reid Dick* in 1967. Royal marriages even at the end of the nineteenth century were a great deal more unsentimental and practical than they appear to be today. By birth, Mary was a princess of Teck in the Kingdom of Württemberg. She was betrothed to George V's elder brother Albert (informally known as Eddy), the Duke of Clarence. He was the future Edward VII's eldest son and heir, and the most sensational and implausible of many candidates suggested at the time for the role of Jack the Ripper, the late

Victorian East End mass murderer. When Eddy died of pneumonia in 1892 at the age of twenty-eight, still unwed, Princess Mary was re-betrothed to Eddy's younger brother George. They were married on 6 July 1893.

Queen Mary has sometimes been criticized for her aggressive acquisition of objets d'art for the Royal Collections in later life. Apocrypha, at least, has it that she would express to her hosts or others her admiration of objects in their possession, in the expectation that the owners would be willing to part with them. Whether there is any substance to this is uncertain. In any case she has to be credited with extensive knowledge of the Royal Collections and with her success in recovering a number of objects that had gone astray over the years, for example by way of loan. She too lived in Marlborough House in her widowhood, which lasted just long enough to permit a poignant photograph of an assembly of three queens – herself, Queen Elizabeth the Queen Mother and Queen Elizabeth II – at the funeral of George VI, respectively their son, husband and father, on 15 February 1952. This was a rare occurrence, there not having been three living queens for nearly 250 years, since the death of Charles II's widow, Catherine of Braganza, in 1705. Mary died on 24 March 1953.

Carry on down The Mall, but only as far as the steps up to Carlton Gardens. Walk to the top of the steps and you will see, dressed in the uniform of an Admiral of the Fleet and Garter robes, *William McMillan's* 1955 bronze of **George VI [11]**. The King is standing, looking out over The Mall.

The King has very recently been joined by his wife, **Queen Elizabeth the Queen Mother [12]**, a 2009 bronze by *Philip Jackson*. The Queen Mother's bronze is very much of a piece with the earlier bronze of the King. She too is in formal Garter robes and is portrayed at her age when the King died, fifty-one. But there are touches of informality in the smile on her face and the hands holding the flowing robes. On each side of the Queen Mother is a bronze **relief panel [13]** by *Paul Day*. On her left as you face the statue is a panel depicting her wartime role, visiting the East End (as she famously said at the time, 'I'm glad we've been bombed [Buckingham Palace was hit during the Blitz]. It makes me feel I can look the East End in the face.'); on the right, a panel depicting her post-war racing successes. The whole ensemble is an elegant combined memorial to the late King and Queen. The single weakness in both the new bronze and the panels is that none of them captures the image of the Queen Mother to the same extent as *McMillan* successfully portrayed the King's face.

Behind **George VI**, on the other side of Carlton Gardens, is *Angela Conner's* 1993 bronze of **General de Gaulle [14]**, portrayed in his 1940 general's uniform and captured in one of those unmistakably characteristic Gaullist shrugs. The first headquarters of the infant Free French Forces from which he made his famous broadcast to the French nation in June 1940 stands only a few yards away, on the other side of the road, behind your right shoulder as you face the statue; the text of his speech is recorded on a plaque on the wall. As a nice coincidence, given the proximity of her own new statue, **de Gaulle** was unveiled by the Queen Mother.

Further down Carlton House Terrace, on the left-hand side, is **Curzon [15]**, a 1931 bronze by *Bertram Mackennal* (you will see more of his work in a moment in Waterloo Place). George Nathaniel Curzon (1859–1925), 'a most superior person' as a contemporary doggerel had it, was: 1st Marquess of Kedleston; Viceroy of India at thirty-nine; Foreign Secretary for five years after the Great War; almost (but not quite) Prime Minister; lover of Elinor Glyn (pioneer of mass-market women's erotic fiction, herself the inadvertent begetter of another contemporary doggerel); voracious restorer of great houses at Walmer, Hackwood, Montacute, Bodiam, and Tattershall, not to mention his own seat of Kedleston; an extraordinary polymath, 'a divinity addressing black beetles'. The statue captures the 'superior person' but misses his sallow, almost Asiatic aura.

Victorians, Edwardians and a Georgian

In Waterloo Place you will find a clutch of largely Victorian worthies, with two later Edwardians and an earlier Georgian. At the top of the steps leading down to The Mall is the earliest of the works, *Richard Westmacott's* 1834 bronze of the **Duke of York [16]**, on his 34-metre (112-foot) high column. Frederick, Duke of York, second son of George III, elected Bishop of Osnaburg at the age of six months and gazetted a major-general at the age of nineteen, is the 'Grand Old Duke of York' immortalized by the nursery rhyme about the ten thousand men, marched up and down hill (during the Duke's spectacularly unsuccessful campaigns in the Low Countries in the 1790s), who 'when they were only half way up they were neither up nor down'. Like his late Victorian successor the Duke of Cambridge, the Duke of York was Commander-in-Chief of the British Army for a prodigiously long time, from 1795 until his death in 1827, with only a brief two-year gap from 1809. The view from the top of his column would be spectacular but, sadly, is inaccessible.

On the west side of Waterloo Place are **Field Marshal Sir John Fox Burgoyne [17]** and **Sir John Franklin [18]**, the former an 1877 bronze by *Edgar Boehm*, the latter a bronze by *Matthew Noble* in 1866. Burgoyne, the first field marshal to emerge from the ranks of the Royal Engineers, was the illegitimate son of General 'Gentleman Johnny' Burgoyne, who surrendered Saratoga during the American War of Independence, and took the 'Fox' from his godfather, Charles James Fox. He made his name as a demolition engineer on Wellington's staff in the Peninsula War and thereafter was principally a construction engineer and effectively Lord Raglan's second-in-command during the Crimean War. He was awarded his field marshal's baton in 1868 at the age of eighty-six – a far from uncommon age in the nineteenth-century era of 'Buggins' turn' (the appointment of a person on the basis of length of service rather than merit or level of qualification) promotion.

Franklin's career, by contrast, was not as successful. He led the disastrous expedition on HM ships *Terror* and *Erebus* in 1845 to find the elusive North-West Passage. Both ships were lost, with all hands, and the fate of the expedition was only finally discovered some fourteen years later. Beyond Franklin, above the entrance to *Decimus Burton's* Athenaeum, is the gleaming gilt copy by *Edward Hodges Baily* of the **Pallas Athene [19]** of Velletri.

On the east side of Waterloo Place is **Robert Scott [20]**, 'Scott of the Antarctic'. Following his death in 1912, this is a 1915 bronze by his widow *Kathleen Scott* (née Bruce and later Lady Kennet), an unlikely Bohemian wife for such an orthodox naval officer. Like the statue of **Florence Nightingale** (see below), which you will see in a moment, this is a rare example of public statuary erected during the Great War. There is a marble replica in Christchurch, New Zealand. Next to **Scott** is *Carlo Marochetti's* figure of **Field Marshal Lord Clyde [21]**, an 1867 bronze on a red granite cylindrical pedestal. As Colin Campbell, Clyde had a distinguished and varied military career, including the command of the Highland Brigade at the Battle of the

Alma during the Crimean War and the command-in-chief in India during the Mutiny. The statue was originally intended for erection on Horse Guards Parade, but on the Admiralty's objection came here instead. Beyond Clyde is another work by *Edgar Boehm* of 1882 – **Sir John (later 1st Lord) Lawrence [22]**, chief administrator of the Punjab during the Mutiny and later Viceroy of India in the 1860s.

In the middle of Waterloo Place, facing the **Guards Crimean Monument** on the other side of Pall Mall, is *Bertram Mackennal's* **Edward VII [23]**, a mounted bronze of 1921 whose plinth still bears the scars of wartime shrapnel damage. *Mackennal* was the first Australian to be elected to the Royal Academy and you can see more of his work on the exterior of Australia House (see page 84). The **Guards Crimean Monument [24]** (see illustration, right) was the work of *John Bell*, and was finished in 1861. The three guardsmen represent the then three Guards regiments, Grenadier, Coldstream and Scots, the Irish and Welsh Guards having been raised only in 1900 and 1914 respectively.

Later additions to the overall 'Crimean' group are the statues of **Sidney Herbert [25]**, by *John Foley* in 1867 and **Florence Nightingale [26]**, by *A. G. Walker* in 1915. **Herbert** was first erected outside the former War Office in Pall Mall and was then moved to the new War Office in Whitehall in 1906. He was Secretary at War during the first part of the Crimean War and instrumental in Florence Nightingale getting out to the Crimea. It seemed only appropriate that he should be moved again to join her here, when her statue was erected in 1915. At the same time, the **Guards Crimean Monument** was shifted 12 metres (39 feet) to the north.

Heading Back to the Mall

Return from the Crimean Monument towards the Duke of York, and turn left along the eastern section of Carlton House Terrace. On the right-hand side is a statue of **Queen Victoria [27]** by *Thomas Brock*. The statue was unveiled by Lord Salisbury in 1902 and was originally sited outside the (now defunct) Constitutional Club. It was moved almost immediately to Wimbledon, from where it returned in 1971 to stand outside what are now the offices of The Crown Estate at numbers 14 and 15.

Walk to the end of Carlton House Terrace and turn right into a small passage. This takes you back down to The Mall. Immediately on the left is a bronze group by *Adrian Jones* in 1903, in honour of the **Royal Marines [28]**. Originally this honoured those marines who fell in South Africa and China in 1899 and 1900, but in 2000 it was rededicated to all fallen marines. Cross over The Mall. With his back to the Admiralty is *Thomas Brock's* 1914 bronze of **Captain James Cook [29]**, the great eighteenth-century naval explorer and navigator. Turn right, towards Buckingham Palace. Around the corner of the Citadel, the visible tip of the huge network of underground bunkers and shelters stretching as far as Marsham Street in Westminster, is the new **National Police Memorial [30]**. It is an austere, black, cuboid shape unveiled in 2005 as a memorial to all British policemen killed in the course of duty and is the work of *Foster & Partners* with the Danish artist *Per Arnoldi*. Walk to the opposite corner of Horse Guards Road to see *Robert Colton's* 1910 **Royal Artillery South African War Memorial [31]**: a bronze Pegasus led by a winged Peace, on a stone pedestal and surround designed by the ubiquitous (in The Mall, at least, where he was also responsible for Admiralty Arch and the facade of Buckingham Palace) *Aston Webb*.

❶ Day and Night
❷ The Winds
❸ Suffragette Memorial
❹ Henry Purcell
❺ Queen Anne
❻ FM Earl Alexander of Tunis
❼ Victoria Memorial
❽ Canadian War Memorial
❾ Queen Alexandra Memorial
❿ Queen Mary
⓫ George VI
⓬ Queen Elizabeth the Queen Mother
⓭ Queen Mother Relief Panels
⓮ General de Gaulle
⓯ Curzon
⓰ Duke of York
⓱ FM Sir John Fox Burgoyne
⓲ Sir John Franklin
⓳ Pallas Athene
⓴ Robert Scott

㉑ FM Lord Clyde
㉒ Sir John Lawrence
㉓ Edward VII
㉔ Guards Crimean Monument
㉕ Sidney Herbert
㉖ Florence Nightingale
㉗ Queen Victoria
㉘ Royal Marines
㉙ Captain James Cook
㉚ National Police Memorial
㉛ Royal Artillery South African War Memorial
㉜ Memorial Fountain to the Royal Naval Divison
㉝ FM Viscount Wolseley
㉞ FM Earl Roberts
㉟ Cadiz Memorial
㊱ FM Earl Kitchener of Khartoum
㊲ Admiral of the Fleet Earl Mountbatten of Burma
㊳ Guards' Monument
㊴ Bali Memorial
㊵ Clive

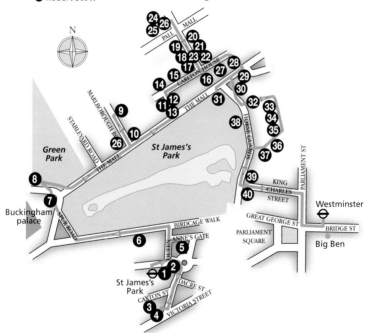

Horse Guards Parade

Walk away from the Mall at the South African War Memorial, and you will come to Horse Guards Parade itself. In the north-west corner is *Edwin Lutyens'* 1925 **Memorial Fountain to the Royal Naval Division [32]**. First installed here on 25 April 1925, on the tenth anniversary of the Gallipoli landings, it was removed from the parade when the Citadel was constructed in 1940. It was subsequently erected at Greenwich in 1951, but was reinstated here in 2003. On the east side, flanking the archway under Horse Guards itself leading through to Whitehall, are equestrian statues of two more great Victorian soldiers: to the north, **Field Marshal Viscount Wolseley [33]** by *William Goscombe John* in 1920 and to the south, **Field Marshal Earl Roberts [34]** by *Henry Poole* in 1924. These two make for an interesting juxtaposition. The army was riven by faction in the late Victorian era and Wolseley was the acknowledged head of the 'Africans' while Roberts led the 'Indians'. The two cordially disliked each other, and it is nicely appropriate that the statues make no eye contact. Wolseley, who succeeded the Duke of Cambridge as Commander-in-Chief in 1895, had earlier fought a succession of small successful Imperial wars, mostly in Africa, and was immortalized by Gilbert and Sullivan, in *The Pirates of Penzance*, as the original of 'the very model of a modern major-general'. The most efficiently organized of soldiers, Wolseley also left us the now sadly archaic expression 'All Sir Garnet', originally army slang meaning 'all is as it should be'.

Roberts, though, is the more interesting statue, and Roberts the man was the more loved and popular soldier. Universally known as 'Bobs', he was Commander-in-Chief first in India, then in South Africa during the main part of the Boer War in 1900, and then of the British Army until the post was abolished in 1904. *Poole's* statue is a reduced version of an 1898 original by *Henry Bates*, who taught *Poole*. Casts of the original are in Glasgow and Calcutta. The horse, which is far more full of energy and realism than **Wolseley's** placid mount, was actually modelled by Roberts' own horse, Volonel.

Beyond **Roberts**, walking towards Downing Street, is the **Cadiz Memorial [35]**, a splendid cast-iron cannon adorned with a monster resembling a Chinese dragon. Made in 1814 at the Woolwich Arsenal to a design by *Robert Shipster*, it was erected in 1816 as a present from Spain to the Prince Regent 'To commemorate the raising of the siege of Cadiz in consequence of the glorious victory gained by the Duke of Wellington over the French near Salamanca 22 July 1812'.

Continue walking round to the south side of Horse Guards Parade. Partly obscured by the trees overhanging the garden wall of 10 Downing Street, is *John Tweed's* 1926 bronze of **Field Marshal Earl Kitchener of Khartoum [36]** – a hatless, standing, contemplative figure. Notwithstanding all his other triumphs and successes – Sirdar of the Egyptian Army, the victor of Omdurman, Commander-in-Chief in South Africa and then in India (where his most successful campaign was his unseating of Curzon from the viceroyalty) – 'K of K', as he was known, is perhaps best remembered, if not indeed immortalized, as the face of the Secretary of State for War in August 1914 on the most famous and successful recruiting poster of all time, 'Your Country Needs You', with that inescapable pointing finger. **Kitchener** was briefly inaccessible behind a seemingly permanent anti-terrorist barrier, but the barrier has now been removed.

To the right of **Kitchener** as you face him, **Admiral of the Fleet Earl Mountbatten of Burma [37]**, by contrast, is now sadly completely isolated behind the new wall and railings around Foreign Office Green. This again is a hatless, standing, informal work, by *Franta Belsky* in

1983, with 'Dickie' holding a large pair of binoculars and surveying the parade ground before him. Around the pedestal are inscribed his many high offices: Supreme Commander in South East Asia, the last Viceroy of India, First Sea Lord (like his father, Prince Louis of Battenberg, forty years earlier) and finally the longest serving Chief of the Defence Staff, before his murder by the IRA in 1979.

Follow round to the west side of Horse Guards Parade to complete the circuit. Here you will find the **Guards' Monument [38]**, *H. C. Bradshaw's* rectangular, sawn-off stone obelisk of 1926, with its five guardsmen in Great War battledress, bronzes by *Gilbert Ledward* all modelled on actual guardsmen from the five regiments of Foot Guards, and with the battle honours and units involved in all the guards' engagements in the Great War inscribed on the stonework. As an emotional work, it is not a patch on *Jagger's* **Royal Artillery Monument** (see page 32), and the five bronze guardsmen seem rather lifeless and wooden. However, it is still an impressive reminder of the guards' sacrifice, here on the edge of the parade ground that hosts the guards' most famous annual pageant, the Trooping the Colour on The Queen's official birthday.

King Charles Street

Turn around and walk back to the south side of Horse Guards Parade and out of the south-west corner on to Horse Guards Road. Walk down the road until you reach the foot of the steps up to King Charles Street on your left. On the left side of the steps is a 2-metre (6 1/2-foot) high stone quadrant, with its outer rim facing the old India Office behind it and the inner rim bearing the monument's inscription. At the centre of the radius of the quadrant is a granite ball, some 1.5 metres (5 feet) in diameter, lightly engraved over its entire surface with doves of peace. The ensemble is 'In memory of the 202 innocent people killed by an act of terrorism in Kuta on the Island of Bali, Indonesia on 12 October 2002', and bears the names of all the 202 victims, from Airlie to Zervos, including those of the 27 Britons killed. The **Bali Memorial [39]** was unveiled by the Prince of Wales on the fourth anniversary of the atrocity.

Walk up the steps. At the top, between the old India Office and the Treasury, stands *John Tweed's* 1912 bronze of **Clive [40]** (see illustration, right) – Robert 1st, Lord Clive, 'Clive of India'. Clive committed suicide in 1774 at the age of only forty-nine after his attempted impeachment by the House of Commons. Originally erected outside Gwydyr House in Whitehall, the statue was moved to its present location in 1916, on the completion of the India Office.

Walk to the end of King Charles Street and turn right into Parliament Street. When you reach Parliament Square turn left into Bridge Street and you will find Westminster Underground Station on your left-hand side.

CLIVE
1725   1774

4. PARLIAMENT AND WHITEHALL – FROM PARLIAMENT SQUARE TO THE ADMIRALTY

START	Westminster Underground Station (Circle, District and Jubilee lines)
FINISH	Charing Cross Underground Station (Northern and Bakerloo lines)
DISTANCE	2 km (1 1/4 miles)
DURATION	45 minutes

This is the shortest walk in the book. It is barely 0.5 km (1/3 mile) as the crow flies from Parliament Square to the Admiralty, but the combination of Parliament Square and Whitehall alone yields one of London's most concentrated collections of public statues. They include a dictator of the English Republic, presidents of the United States of America and the Union of South Africa, two kings, six field marshals, eight prime ministers and a great deal more besides.

London's Famous Timekeeper

As you emerge from Westminster Underground Station on to Bridge Street (straight ahead, as you pass through the tube barrier), you are almost underneath that quintessential icon of London, the Clock Tower of the Palace of Westminster. This 1830's masterpiece of *Barry* (*Charles* and *Edward* – father and son) and *Pugin* is known (wrongly) around the world as Big Ben. Strictly that name belongs to the hour bell of the Great Clock, the 13.5-ton monster cast in 1859 by the Whitechapel Bell Foundry. The foundry is Britain's oldest continuous manufacturing company. It cast its first bell in 1570 during the reign of Queen Elizabeth and is still flourishing today. Turn right at the tube exit, and at the corner of Bridge Street and Parliament Street a plaque above the Parliamentary Bookshop records that this junction was the site of London's first traffic lights, as long ago as 1868. It was a pretty rudimentary machine, operated manually by a policeman, but also a comforting reminder, perhaps, that traffic jams have not been the monopoly of the twentieth and twenty-first centuries.

South of Parliament Square

Before you head off in the direction of Whitehall, you are going to take a brief detour in the opposite direction. Leave Parliament Square by its south-east corner and walk down St Margaret's Place, which runs into Old Palace Yard and then into Abingdon Street. Turning to your left, enter Victoria Tower Gardens on the south side of the Palace of Westminster, which is the formal name of the Houses of Parliament. In the middle of the gardens is a cast of *Auguste Rodin's* **Burghers of Calais** [1], presented to the nation in 1914 by the National Art Collections Fund, then as now the principal private sector saviour of works of art from exile abroad.

At the entrance to the gardens, in the shadow of the Victoria Tower, is *A. G. Walker's* bronze of **Mrs (Emmeline) Pankhurst [2]** (see illustration, below), the principal and most famous campaigner for female suffrage. Her daughter, Dame Christabel Pankhurst, is commemorated by a bronze medallion on one of the flanking piers. Partial female suffrage for women over thirty was granted in 1918, but universal and equal suffrage only came in 1928, which was also the year of Mrs Pankhurst's death. Her statue was unveiled in 1930 by Stanley Baldwin, then both former and future Prime Minister. *Walker* was also responsible for London's first female non-royal public statue, of **Florence Nightingale** (see page 40).

Come out of the gardens and cross over the road to Abingdon Green. Here you will see a rare sculptural exception to the concentrated feast of statuary on this walk – *Henry Moore's* **Knife Edge Two Piece [3]**, a second cast in 1967 of his original 1962 abstract work. Staying on the same side of the road, move on from the green and walk northwards towards Parliament Square. After a few yards you will find **George V [4]**, a 1947 work in Portland stone by *William Reid Dick*. The King is in Garter robes and field marshal's uniform; an inappropriate choice, perhaps, for a monarch with a closer active association with (and service in) the Royal Navy than any other king since William IV.

Almost opposite this sombre work on the other side of the road is a complete contrast, *Carlo Marochetti's* magnificently exuberant **Richard Coeur de Lion [5]**, the Lionheart, England's twelfth-century crusading (and consequently largely absent) king. *Marochetti* was an Italian who came to London after the French Revolution of 1848, with a barony conferred by the King of Sardinia. **Richard** was originally displayed as a plaster work at the Great Exhibition of 1851, and was only later cast and erected here in 1860. He appears every inch the crusader, or alternatively simply 'completely over the top'.

Cross back over the road to Westminster Abbey. **Richard** is opposite the Chapel of Henry VII, at the east end of the abbey. The sixteen gilt weather vanes on the roof of the chapel were given by the Royal Institution of Chartered Surveyors (RICS) to mark the centenary of the RICS's Royal Charter in 1981. The collective gratitude of the Dean and Chapter is inscribed on a stone **[6]** in the wall at the east end, followed by this delightfully apt verse from Ecclesiastes 1:6 – 'The wind goeth toward the south, and turneth about unto the north; it whirleth about continually, and the wind returneth again according to his circuits.'

The Periphery of Parliament Square
Cross over the road and walk back up to the south-east corner of Parliament Square.

Overlooking this corner, with his back to Westminster Hall, is *Hamo Thornycroft's* 1899 bronze of **Oliver Cromwell [7]**. In the earlier part of the 1890s an attempt at promoting a Parliament-sponsored statue of Cromwell, to commemorate the tercentenary of his birth, had foundered on a combination of the strong opposition of Irish members and the fall of the then Liberal government headed by the Earl of Rosebery. The statue was nevertheless commissioned and executed, thanks to Rosebery's subsequent private intervention in the barely concealed guise of 'an anonymous donor'. Not inappropriately, **Cromwell** has his back turned to Parliament, which was dissolved and ignored during the last years of the English Republic, or Commonwealth: that brief period of barely a dozen years when, uniquely since Roman times, England has not been ruled as a monarchy.

In facing west, however, with his head slightly bowed, **Cromwell** looks directly at a small lead bust of **Charles I [8]**, who was executed by Cromwell's republican regime on 30 January 1649 – the only English regicide since the death of Richard III at the Battle of Bosworth Field in 1485, when the Plantagenet line of kings yielded to the Tudors. Cross over St Margaret's Street and take a closer look at it. It is mounted in a niche in the east wall of St Margaret's Church. It is by an unknown sculptor of around 1800 and was found in a builder's yard after the Second World War. It was placed in its current location in 1950, a nicely ironic touch.

The West of Parliament Square

On the west side of Parliament Square is **Abraham Lincoln [9]**, sixteenth President of the United States and the most illustrious of all the nineteenth-century Presidents. Britain and the United States had last been at war with each other as long ago as 1815 (the year in which British troops burnt the White House) and the delightfully named American Committee for the Celebration of the Hundredth Anniversary of Peace Among English-Speaking Peoples first proposed in 1914 the offer of a statue of Lincoln for Parliament Square, to mark the then forthcoming centenary. War between the English-speaking and the German-speaking peoples intervened, however, and the proposal was shelved until 1920, when the present replica of *Auguste Saint-Gauden's* Chicago Lincoln Memorial was presented by the US Government.

Behind Lincoln is the old **Middlesex Guildhall [10]**, latterly the Middlesex Crown Court and the intended home of the new Supreme Court when the Law Lords – the ultimate appeal court in Britain – move out of the House of Lords. The historical figure frieze and statuary around the portal, on the east frontage facing the square, are by *Henry C. Fehr* and date from the Guildhall's construction in 1912–13.

To Lincoln's left in 'Canning Enclosure' is *Richard Westmacott's* 1832 bronze of **George Canning [11]**. Canning was twice Foreign Secretary and briefly Prime Minister in 1827 (after Lord Liverpool's long, fifteen-year tenure) before his death that year at the early age of fifty-seven. The statue was first erected in New Palace Yard, beside the House of Commons, but was moved here in 1867 in anticipation of the construction of the District Line. Like *Westmacott's* slightly earlier depiction of **Charles James Fox** in Bloomsbury (see page 114), this is a classical, idealized work, with Canning in a Roman toga, unlike his conventionally dressed peers.

The Centre of Parliament Square

In the middle of the square are another president, seven prime ministers (one non-British) and a field marshal, although one of the prime ministers doubles up as the field marshal. In the south-west corner, nearest the abbey, is one of the two newest arrivals in the square, *Ian Walters'* 2007 bronze of **Nelson Mandela [12]** (see illustration, right), first President of post-apartheid South Africa and probably less in need of introduction than anyone else mentioned in this book. He is depicted in his trademark flamboyant, high-collared shirt. *Walters* died before the actual bronze was cast; indeed the statue had been a protracted and contentious affair. The sculptor and its promoters – the South African newspaper editor (the late) Donald Woods, Richard Attenborough and the then Mayor of London, Ken Livingstone – wanted it to be in Trafalgar Square, which Westminster City Council successfully resisted, and it took the best part of five years to get the statue erected here. It was unveiled on 29 August 2007, in the presence of Mandela himself, with the square full of delighted spectators. *Walters*, by the way, also sculpted the bronze head of Mandela that sits by the south side of the Festival Hall. This gives Mandela the further distinction of being the only person other than Queen Victoria to be commemorated more than once on the streets of London by the same sculptor.

Immediately next to Mandela is *Matthew Noble's* 1877 bronze of **Sir Robert Peel [13]**, from the re-cast bronze of *Marochetti's* earlier statue of Peel in New Palace Yard that was removed after a Parliamentary vote in 1868. Though he was Prime Minister and a distinguished Tory statesman, Peel is best remembered today as the founder of the modern Metropolitan Police Force. It is from Peel that the nickname 'bobby' for a police constable is derived. In a historical sense, Peel is perhaps more fittingly commemorated by his earlier 1853 statue, by *William Calder Marshall*, in Piccadilly Gardens, Manchester, where he is nicely paired with *Matthew Noble's* own 1856 statue of the other great Tory statesman of Peel's era, the Duke of Wellington.

Next to Peel is **Benjamin Disraeli, Earl of Beaconsfield [14]**, one of the most remarkable men ever to have held the office of British Prime Minister. He was Jewish by birth (he was baptized as a Christian at an early age by his father, but was still '*der alte Jude*', 'the old Jew', to Bismarck sixty years later); he was a solicitor, novelist, populist, statesman, re-founder of the modern Tory Party after its disintegration on the fall of Peel's government, and Queen Victoria's favourite Prime Minister. It is a bronze by *Mario Rossi* in 1883, two years after Disraeli's death. The Queen herself sent a funeral wreath of primroses from Osborne marked 'his favourite flower' and the Primrose League, which was founded in Disraeli's honour, was for over a century after his death a flourishing organization for the propagation of Conservative principles and aspirations. Each anniversary of his death (on 19 April) until the Great War was marked by the garlanding of the statue with quantities of primroses.

In the north-west corner is the **Earl of Derby [15]**, Disraeli's immediate predecessor as Tory Prime Minister and a Victorian *magnifico* long eclipsed by his successor. This is an 1874 bronze, also by *Matthew Noble*, and was unveiled by Disraeli himself.

In front of **Derby**, on the north side and facing south, is **Viscount Palmerston [16]**, one of the most long-lived – and with Disraeli, one of the most popular – nineteenth-century statesmen. He became Secretary at War in 1809 (he held this office until 1828, under five different prime ministers), he was Foreign Secretary between 1830 and 1851 save during Peel's two administrations and twice Prime Minister between 1855 and his death in 1865. This is a work by *Thomas Woolner* in 1876.

Next to **Palmerston** is *Jacob Epstein's* 1956 bronze of **Jan Smuts [17]**, a Boer and consequently an enemy of Imperial Britain. Yet after the settlement of the Boer War he became a soldier, lawyer, statesman, Imperialist, Prime Minister of South Africa, British field marshal, member of the British War Cabinet in two world wars and Chancellor of Cambridge University. Smuts is in field marshal's uniform, poised rather precariously forward, on a pedestal of South African granite. Contrast this with *Epstein's* **Rima** (see page 19) of thirty years earlier: sculptor and subject each turned from *enfant terrible* to pillar of the Establishment.

To **Smuts'** left is the most recent arrival in the square, *Glynn Williams'* 2007 bronze of **David Lloyd George [18]**. By comparison with all the other statesmen in the Square, this is a crude and uncharacteristic representation of one of the two great British war leaders of the twentieth century. It

CHURCHILL

is more akin to an eccentric professor or a benign magician than to a very distinguished, and complicated, Prime Minister. (*William Goscombe John's* statue in the shadow of Caernarvon Castle is a rather more evocative portrayal.)

The last statue in the square itself is the massive bulk of *Ivor Roberts-Jones's* bronze of **Churchill [19]** (see illustration, left), unveiled by Lady Churchill in 1973. It is the complete antithesis of the previous statue in its impressively successful portrayal of the man. For *Roberts-Jones* it must in one sense have been the most daunting of commissions. How do you portray and do full justice to the most famous Englishman of all time? (Churchill's only rival for that accolade is Shakespeare, see page 104). This site, at the north-east corner of the central island, had already been chosen by Churchill himself. One of the greatest of all parliamentarians, he stands directly opposite, and facing, the Houses of Parliament (the only consequent discordant note is that his back is turned to **Smuts**, which is something that the living Churchill would never have done). The 3.6-metre (12-foot) bronze, on its 2.4-metre (8-foot) pedestal, is informal, but also absolutely indomitable. It is the portrayal of Churchill the war leader, the saviour of Britain in 1940, at the moment when, in his own words on becoming Prime Minister, '...all my past life had been a preparation for this hour and this trial...' The statue depicts a military greatcoat, but it is still a hatless civilian. By contrast, Churchill's Parisian statue – in the Avenue Winston Churchill, of course – is in RAF uniform.

Heading to Whitehall

On the north side of the square, with its main frontage facing on to Parliament Street, is the **Treasury** [20], a largely Edwardian neo-Baroque building. Your only interest is in the modest sculpture in the pediment over the main entrance, so leave the Square by the north-east corner and walk up Parliament Street on the east, right-hand side and take a look. It is by *Bertram Mackennal*.

Carry on walking in the same direction and just past King Charles Street is the architecturally and sculpturally more interesting **Foreign and Commonwealth Office [21]**, whose principal architect was *George Gilbert Scott*. Built in 1870–5, these buildings originally housed the Home Office and the Colonial Office (to see the old India Office and Foreign Office do the walk on pages 34–45). At ground level reliefs of various muses and similar figures represent Victorian virtues and the continents of the world. At the upper level are relief busts of assorted monarchs and distinguished Englishmen. Many sculptors were employed, notably *H. H. Armstead* and *J. Birnie Philip*.

Whitehall

Continue walking up Parliament Street and where it turns into Whitehall proper is the **Cenotaph** [22], Britain's national war memorial, situated on an island in the middle of the road. It is the work of *Edwin Lutyens* in 1919–20 and is arguably his finest work in London. For the first commemoration of the 1918 armistice in 1919, the Cenotaph was merely a wooden construction, but that temporary structure was widely praised and it was repeated and replaced before the second anniversary by the present Portland-stone edifice. There is no effigy nor any mark of religion. There are also no horizontal or vertical lines. With due classical entasis, the apparent horizontals are convex to a point about 273 metres (896 feet) underground and the apparent verticals meet about 304 metres (997 feet) above. The concept of the empty tomb as a memorial was an original idea of *Lutyens* himself. The flags on both the long sides are an integral part of the design, as is *Lutyens'* own later addition (in 1938) of the demountable railings on the south side that appear at the armistice service every year. The **Cenotaph** is one of the most moving monuments in London.

Immediately to the north of the **Cenotaph**, and also on an island in the middle of the road is **Women in War [23]**, a 2005 edifice sculpted by *John W. Mills*. A large, plain, bronze cuboid, it is adorned with various different items of female overclothing, military and civilian, apparently symbolizing the contribution of women to Britain's war effort in the Second World War. It is difficult to dispel first impressions of a fossilized and untidy outdoor cloakroom, and the strong feeling that this mundanely expressed memorial has no business in the grandeur of Whitehall.

Stay on the east side of Whitehall. Opposite **Women in War** you will find a trio of field marshals with their backs to the Ministry of Defence – from south to north, **Montgomery**, **Alanbrooke** and **Slim**. **Field Marshal Viscount Montgomery of Alamein [24]** is a 1980 bronze by *Oscar Nemon*, while **Field Marshals Viscounts Alanbrooke [25]** and **Slim [26]** are both by *Ivor Roberts-Jones*, unveiled in 1993 and 1990 respectively. All three are in successfully evocative and characteristic poses: Montgomery, the best-known of all Britain's Second World War generals ('in defeat unbeatable, in victory unbearable', in Churchill's words); Alanbrooke 'The Master of Strategy' (as his pedestal is inscribed) and the only man able to restrain some of Churchill's dottier military impulses during the war; and Slim, the soldiers' general, as modest as he was successful in the appalling conditions of Burma.

Sadly *William McMillan's* 1959 delightful little sub-life-size bronze of **Sir Walter Raleigh**, which used to stand here on the corner of the green, was moved to Greenwich in 2001, but you will see it in the final walk (see page 138).

Continue walking northwards, past Gwydyr House, a late eighteenth-century building now housing the Welsh Office, and past *Inigo Jones's* largest surviving masterpiece in central London, the Banqueting House, from one of whose great windows Charles I walked out on to his scaffold on 30 January 1649. An anonymous bust of **Charles I [27]** over the ground floor entrance to the Banqueting House commemorates the King's execution.

On another island in the middle of the road, opposite the Banqueting House, is **Field Marshal Earl Haig [28]**, the Commander-in-Chief of the British Armies in France from 1915–18. This 1937 bronze by *Alfred Hardiman* combines a naturalistic (if also surprisingly and uncharacteristically, hatless) rider and a sepulchrally stylized horse. Haig, very much the cavalryman, is portrayed on much more plausibly satisfactory mounts outside Edinburgh Castle and in Montreuil in northern France where he had his general headquarters – the latter statue having been recently rescued from its obscure backstreet site and re-erected before the town theatre.

A Detour off Whitehall

At the traffic lights by Horse Guards Parade, the 1750s complex originally designed by *William Kent* and the traditional headquarters of the British Army until the twentieth century, take a right turn into Horse Guards Avenue. At the junction is *Herbert Hampton's* 1911 bronze of the 8th **Duke of Devonshire [29]**, better known during the larger part of his public life, before he inherited the dukedom, by his courtesy title of Lord Hartington. With Joseph Chamberlain, he was the leader of the Liberal Unionists in the House of Commons who joined Lord Salisbury's Tories when Gladstone split the Liberal Party with his Irish Home Rule Bill of 1886. 'Harty Tarty' was a byword for independence and absolute incorruptibility, and three times refused Queen Victoria's invitation to become Prime Minister.

Continue along Horse Guards Avenue and you will come to the north entrance of the huge Ministry of Defence, first conceived in the early 1930s but only completed in 1959. Above the entrance are two massive sculptures of **Earth** and **Water [30]** by *Charles Wheeler*, each carved from 40 tons of Portland stone. **Fire** and **Air** above the corresponding south entrance were vetoed by the Treasury. Opposite the north entrance, at the junction with Whitehall Court, is a 1997 copy of *Richard Goulden's* 1924 **Gurkha Rifleman [31]**, whose original is at Kunraghat in India. Cross over the road and take a look. The inscription reads: 'Bravest of the brave, Most generous of the generous, Never had country, More faithful friends than you'.

Walk up Whitehall Court to the **Royal Tank Regiment Memorial [32]**, by *Vivien Mallock* in 2000 after a design by *G. H. Paulin*. The memorial is five tank crewmen in a row, from a 1945 Comet tank, on the slimmest of plinths, described by Pevsner '...as if alert to what might trundle round the corner'. The plinth bears the inscription, 'From Mud through Blood, to the Green Fields Beyond'.

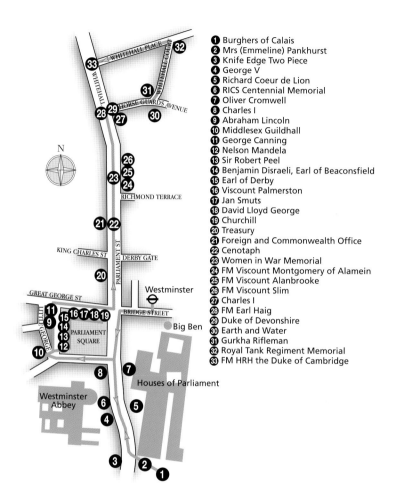

1 Burghers of Calais
2 Mrs (Emmeline) Pankhurst
3 Knife Edge Two Piece
4 George V
5 Richard Coeur de Lion
6 RICS Centennial Memorial
7 Oliver Cromwell
8 Charles I
9 Abraham Lincoln
10 Middlesex Guildhall
11 George Canning
12 Nelson Mandela
13 Sir Robert Peel
14 Benjamin Disraeli, Earl of Beaconsfield
15 Earl of Derby
16 Viscount Palmerston
17 Jan Smuts
18 David Lloyd George
19 Churchill
20 Treasury
21 Foreign and Commonwealth Office
22 Cenotaph
23 Women in War Memorial
24 FM Viscount Montgomery of Alamein
25 FM Viscount Alanbrooke
26 FM Viscount Slim
27 Charles I
28 FM Earl Haig
29 Duke of Devonshire
30 Earth and Water
31 Gurkha Rifleman
32 Royal Tank Regiment Memorial
33 FM HRH the Duke of Cambridge

Return to Whitehall

Turn left into Whitehall Place and walk back to Whitehall (thereby completing your inadvertent circumnavigation of the Old War Office). In the middle of the road between the Old War Office and Horse Guards Parade you will see *Adrian Jones's* 1907 bronze of **Field Marshal HRH the Duke of Cambridge [33]**. He was the grandson of George III and for nearly forty years from 1856 to 1895 he was the Commander-in-Chief of the British Army. This is a lifelike and energetic statue, in marked contrast to the one representing **Haig** (see above), and typical of *Jones's* mastery of equestrian sculpture.

Turn right and walk up Whitehall to Trafalgar Square. Walk around the square in an anticlockwise direction and you will see entrances to Charing Cross Underground Station in the south-east corner of the square itself, and immediately outside the south corner of South Africa House.

5. FIVE SQUARES AND A CIRCUS – FROM SOHO SQUARE TO TRAFALGAR SQUARE

START	Tottenham Court Road Underground Station (Central and Northern (Charing Cross branch) lines.
FINISH	Charing Cross Underground Station (Northern and Bakerloo lines)
DISTANCE	4 km (2 1/2 miles)
DURATION	1 ¼ hour

At the heart of a great city like London, it is no surprise that all these walks pass through squares and other *ronds-points*. This walk is a little different, in that it is largely concentrated on five squares and a circus. Even though the first two squares have only a solitary statue apiece, they are worth the visit, being two of central London's older surviving squares. From the architectural charms of Carolean London, you will proceed through some of the more colourful, even risqué, parts of Soho, and then theatre- and film-land, before ending at the Victorian grandeur of Trafalgar Square.

The formal open spaces and vistas of Trafalgar Square will seem very remote at the start of the walk: traffic, pedestrians, bustle and sleazy shops at the eastern end of Oxford Street; the narrow streets in Soho, whose name may be derived from an old hunting call, 'So-Ho'. When you emerge from Tottenham Court Road Underground Station (take the exit marked 'Oxford Street South Side'), walk a short distance west along Oxford Street before turning left down Soho Street towards Soho Square.

Soho Square

Soho Square was first laid out for building in the reign of Charles II, in 1677, and although it has suffered the fate of most London squares and now contains an eclectic collection of buildings spanning three centuries, some original seventeenth-century buildings still survive.

On the north side of the square's gardens, facing you as you enter from Soho Street, is **Charles II** [1] himself, a marble by *Caius Gabriel Cibber*, who was the father of Colley Cibber, former Poet Laureate (and whose embellishment of **The Monument** you can see if you complete the walk on pages 91–99). The statue was originally erected in 1681, on a pedestal, as part of a larger monument in the centre of the square comprising a fountain and basin and four figures representing English rivers. The whole ensemble was removed in 1876, and in the early twentieth century the kitsch 'Hansel and Gretel' pavilion was erected on the spot vacated by the departed monarch. The statue itself was returned to the square in 1938, as the gift of Lady Gilbert, the widow of W. S. Gilbert (dramatist and librettist), but without its plinth and other supporting sculpture it looks in every sense pedestrian and un-regal. It is also in very poor repair – the Moth-eaten, rather than the Merry, Monarch. (To see a more regal and better preserved statue of **Charles II**, see page 123.)

Golden Square

Now you have some nifty navigational wiggling to do. In every street you will find a hotchpotch of architectural styles and ages – twentieth-century eyesores, seventeenth-century gems and all shades in-between. Leave Soho Square on its west side and walk a short way along Carlisle Street. Turn left into Dean Street, then right into St Anne's Court, which will bring you to Wardour Street; turn left into Wardour Street, then right into Broadwick Street; walk along Broadwick Street and turn left into Marshall Street. Walk along until you hit Beak Street, turn right into Beak Street and then almost immediately on your left on the other side of the street you will see your next stop, Golden Square. Cross over the road and walk into the square. In Golden Square itself you will find another monarch's statue, again in stone and again having suffered severe deterioration before a very inadequate restoration in the 1980s. This is **George II [2]**, in Roman costume, and it was erected here in 1753: the definitive authorship is uncertain, but it is attributed to *John Nost*, and is said to have been made in the 1720s for Canons, the 1st Duke of Chandos's palace in Middlesex. (This king has suffered nearly as much dilapidation in his other public monument, which you can see in the walk on pages 130–141.)

Leave Golden Square by its south-west corner, where a blue plaque records that these, the oldest and most pleasing buildings in the square, include the residence of the Portuguese Embassy between 1724 and 1747.

St James's Square

Turn left into Lower John Street, cross over Brewer Street and into Air Street, which leads down to Piccadilly. Cross to the south side of Piccadilly, and then proceed westwards. To reach Jermyn Street, we may pass through the temptations of the former Simpson's, now Waterstones, London's largest bookshop after Foyles in Charing Cross Road, or through *Wren's* St James's, Piccadilly – itself well worth a visit inside, and with minor statuary by *Charles Wheeler* and *Alfred Hardiman* in the small churchyard on the Piccadilly side. From Jermyn Street, turn into Duke of York Street and St James's Square at the bottom. Although there are no surviving seventeenth-century houses, this is in fact an even older square than either of the first two stops, having been first laid out in 1665. The present garden layout in the centre is largely the work in 1817–18 of *John Nash*.

In the centre of the square is another monarch, but this time in the more substantial form of a well-preserved bronze. This is **William III [3]**, mounted and in classical dress, a work begun by *John Bacon Sr* in 1794 and finished by his son *John Bacon Jr* before being erected here in 1808. Under the left rear hoof of the horse is the famous molehill commemorated by the Jacobite toast 'To the little gentleman in black velvet'. William, already in poor health in the last winter of his life, fell when his horse Sorrel stumbled on a molehill while hunting at Hampton Court, and died shortly afterwards. Although not directly responsible for the King's death, the humble mole was held in high affection by the exiled supporters of his deposed predecessor, James II, and his descendants.

Like **Charles II** in Soho Square, **William III** was surrounded by a circular basin until the 1850s. The statue briefly departed from the square and spent the Second World War at Berkhamsted Castle with an assortment of statuary, including **George III**, **Field Marshal Lord Wolseley** and the **Burghers of Calais**.

In the south-west corner is the square's only other sculpture, **The Stag [4]** – very much at bay – by *Marcus Cornish* of 2001. Leave the square on the east side. Walk along Charles II Street and then turn left into Lower Regent Street and walk towards Piccadilly Circus.

A London Icon and a Rarity

At Piccadilly Circus, on what since 1986 has become a pedestrian peninsula rather than a traffic-encompassed island, is the **Shaftesbury Memorial**, better known simply as 'Eros' [5], perhaps the best-known and certainly the most photographed statuary icon of London. It is a rare example, at least on these walks, of an aluminium work: the lightness of the metal permits the remarkable, almost airborne, posture of Eros. It is the work of *Alfred Gilbert* in 1893, and may seem to us today to be something of a paradox, with a representation of the pagan god of erotic love commemorating one of the great Victorian evangelical Christian reformers, Anthony Ashley Cooper, 7th Earl of Shaftesbury. 'Eros' was briefly moved to Victoria Embankment Gardens in 1925, to permit the construction of the Underground station, returning in 1931. It spent the Second World War in Egham, but otherwise has been an indelible part of the image of Piccadilly Circus for over a century. In the mid-1980s, the statue was restored by George Mancini, who had worked for *Gilbert* as a young man. If any single statue epitomizes London, it is 'Eros'.

Head east from 'Eros', walking to the right of the statue past the Criterion Restaurant to the corner of Haymarket. Here you will see one of the few consistently spouting fountains in London, adorned by four bronze **Horses of Helios [6]**, a 1992 work by *Rudy Weller*.

Leicester Square

Cross over Haymarket and into Coventry Street. Keep walking along this street and you will come to Leicester Square. Walk into the gardens in the centre of the square. Originally named Leicester Fields, it was first laid out as a square in the late seventeenth century by the then Earl of Leicester. As a social address, it saw its heyday in the eighteenth century. It was at Leicester House, on the north side of the square, that Frederick Prince of Wales, son of George II and father of George III, achieved a sort of immortality in 1751 by dying as cricket's first famous fatality, having been struck by a cricket ball. But it was always a more modest square than St James's Square, and went steeply downhill, socially speaking, in the mid-nineteenth century after Cranbourn and Coventry Streets were opened up. Residential use gave way to today's commerce and by the early 1870s the middle of the square was a barren rubbish dump. Rescue came from a surprising quarter. 'Baron' Albert Grant was an Irishman who became a highly successful, slick company promoter, floating all sorts of exotically named and often worthless companies to gullible investors. He became a Member of Parliament and even received a barony from King Victor Emmanuel for services rendered to the Italian House of Savoy. A colourful character, to say the least, he nevertheless rendered one real service to London by purchasing the neglected square and paying for its layout as a public garden, before presenting the finished square to the Metropolitan Board of Works in 1874.

The centrepiece of Grant's gift, whose layout was designed by *James Knowles Jr*, is the **Shakespeare Monument [7]** in the centre of the gardens, described with some justice by Pevsner as 'the most unpretentious that a capital has ever put up to the greatest national poet'. The statue, by *Giovanni Fontana*, copied from *Peter Scheemakers's* 1741 statue of the Bard in Westminster Abbey, is so unassuming in its location that it is hard to believe that it is a tribute to the greatest man in English literature. Shakespeare stands with his legs crossed, and he is leaning on a pile of books bearing the legend 'There is no darkness but ignorance'.

At the four corners of the gardens are very shabby stone busts of famous Englishmen with ostensible connections with the square: in the north-west corner, **Sir Joshua Reynolds [8]**, by *Henry*

Weekes; to the north-east, **William Hogarth [9]**, by *Joseph Durham*; to the south-east, **John Hunter [10]** (the pre-eminent eighteenth-century anatomist and surgeon), by *Thomas Woolner;* and in the south-west corner, **Sir Isaac Newton [11]**, by *William Calder Marshall.* This is a distinguished quartet, even if only Reynolds and Hunter can claim firm connections with the square, by virtue of having had their houses on the west and east side respectively during their later years. All these works are from 1874–5.

Nowadays Leicester Square is synonymous with 'filmland' in London and any big film worth its salt will be premiered in one of the great cinemas on three of the four sides of the square. It is therefore appropriate that the last statue in the square, and its only bronze, is a small sub-life-size representation of the young **Charlie Chaplin [12]** (see illustration, below) by *John Doubleday*

57

in 1981 – the 'little man' with trademark hat and stick from his early days with the Keystone Company under Mack Sennett, of *Mack and Mabel* fame. It was unveiled by the distinguished twentieth-century knight of the stage, Sir Ralph Richardson.

From One Square to Another

You are now going to take a slightly circuitous route between the fourth and fifth squares on this walk and take in five very different works before arriving at Trafalgar Square. Leave Leicester Square by its south-east corner into Irving Street, which brings you (appropriately enough) to *Thomas Brock's* 1910 bronze of **Sir Henry Irving [13]**, in the small triangular piazzetta on the north side of the National Portrait Gallery. As Garrick and Gielgud were unrivalled on the eighteenth- and twentieth-century stages, so did Irving command the theatrical stage of the later part of the nineteenth century. The most remarkable feature of Irving's statue is not the likeness – which, from photographs and his portrait in the Garrick Club, seems a very good one – so much as the fact that this is the only thespian statue in central London apart from **Chaplin**, its nearest companions being the marble of Mrs Siddons, of the previous century, on Paddington Green, and the recently arrived bronze of Laurence Olivier outside the National Theatre on the South Bank.

Cross the road to St Martin's Place, the junction of Charing Cross Road and St Martin's Lane. From a great stage tragedian to a real-life tragic heroine, in the shape of *George Frampton's* 1920 marble of **Edith Cavell [14]** (see illustration, right), standing austerely and looking with unflinching gaze past her executioners to Trafalgar Square and beyond. Edith Cavell, a British nurse trapped in Brussels by the advance of the German armies in 1914, was subsequently arrested by the Germans for helping British and French soldiers to escape, and was shot by a firing squad on 12 October 1915. Her execution was widely condemned as barely judicialized murder and was one of the more notorious examples of the 'barbarism of the Hun' during the Great War. After the war, in 1919, she was exhumed and reburied in Norwich Cathedral. The famous inscription on the plinth reads 'Patriotism is not enough. I must have no hatred or bitterness for anyone', which were among her last words, recorded by the English priest who was with her the night before her execution.

Head into William IV Street, then take a right into Adelaide Street. Just along this street, at the eastern end of St Martin-in-the-Fields church, you will find something completely different: *Maggi Hambling's* 1998 bronze of **Oscar Wilde [15]**. It is a head, smoking a cigarette, at one end of a low granite plinth that also serves as a bench. It is Wilde, emerging from a sarcophagus, living on, pretty much down in the gutter, accessible to passers-by. Indeed, it is called 'A Conversation with Oscar Wilde', should you choose to stop and have one with him. The plinth quotes Wilde: 'We are all in the gutter, but some of us are looking at the stars'. You will either love or loathe it. You are now going to proceed from this head without a body to a group of bodies without heads.

Continue to Duncannon Street, turn left and walk up the Strand to Number 429, the rather grim, grey, granite and stone building on the corner of Agar Street and the Strand. This is **Zimbabwe House [16]**, originally built for the British Medical Association in 1908. Here you will find *Jacob Epstein's* eighteen sculpted nudes, carved in situ, framing the second-floor windows. Representing the **Ages of Man**, in their pristine state they apparently provoked

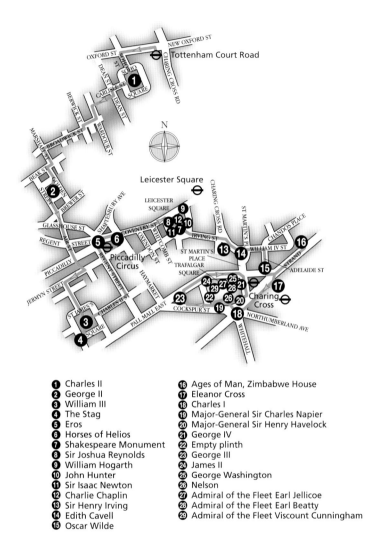

1 Charles II
2 George II
3 William III
4 The Stag
5 Eros
6 Horses of Helios
7 Shakespeare Monument
8 Sir Joshua Reynolds
9 William Hogarth
10 John Hunter
11 Sir Isaac Newton
12 Charlie Chaplin
13 Sir Henry Irving
14 Edith Cavell
15 Oscar Wilde

16 Ages of Man, Zimbabwe House
17 Eleanor Cross
18 Charles I
19 Major-General Sir Charles Napier
20 Major-General Sir Henry Havelock
21 George IV
22 Empty plinth
23 George III
24 James II
25 George Washington
26 Nelson
27 Admiral of the Fleet Earl Jellicoe
28 Admiral of the Fleet Earl Beatty
29 Admiral of the Fleet Viscount Cunningham

strong critical reaction, but it is difficult to appreciate that today. Unfortunately the porous stone of the sculptures was susceptible to the ravages of the weather and bits started to drop off, to the consternation of passers-by below. This occurred to such an extent that in 1937 all the limbs and protuberances of the carvings were hacked off, leaving the mutilated remains that you see today.

Cross over to the other side of the Strand and walk back in the direction you came in until you reach Charing Cross Station. In front of the station stands a curio, which is an 1865 reproduction, designed by *E. M. Barry* and carved by *Thomas Earp*, of the 1293 **Eleanor Cross** **[17]**, the last of the memorials erected by Edward I to mark the route of the funeral cortege of his queen, Eleanor, from Nottingham to Westminster Abbey. The original, destroyed in 1647, stood roughly on the site now occupied by **Charles I**, whom you will see in a moment. Like the Martyrs' Memorial in Oxford, there is a faint suggestion of the iceberg-like tip of the spire of a sunken cathedral.

Trafalgar Square

Turn left out of Charing Cross Station and continue walking down the Strand until you arrive at the south-east corner of Trafalgar Square. Immediately before you at the bottom of the square, now on its own traffic island and only recently thoroughly restored, is one of London's oldest public statues, and certainly its oldest equestrian bronze, *Hubert Le Sueur's* **Charles I [18]** of 1633. *Le Sueur* was French, as his name suggests, and an expert in bronze casting. Remarkably, for a contemporary statue of a living monarch, it was a private commission by Lord Weston, later 1st Earl of Portland, although clearly it was a commission with royal approval, since Portland had succeeded the Duke of Buckingham as the King's favourite minister by that time, and this must have been a project intended to enhance Charles's monarchical prestige. The statue suffered various vicissitudes during the Civil War and Commonwealth, including at one stage being buried underground for safekeeping. But it survived and was reacquired by the Portland family after the Restoration of 1660. Charles II purchased it from the Duchess of Portland in 1675 and erected it on its present site. It has received quite major restoration since the turn of the millennium and now looks in remarkably good condition.

Behind **Charles I**, at the south-west and south-east corners of the square itself, are a couple more Victorian soldiers. To the left is **Major-General Sir Charles Napier [19]** by *G. G. Adams* in 1855. Napier (not to be confused with Field Marshal Lord Napier of Magdala) was a great-great grandson of Charles II and a cousin of Charles James Fox. His genealogical pedigree aside, his main claim to our interest is almost certainly apocryphal. At the conclusion of his successful conquest of Sind (in India) in 1843, he is said to have sent the one-word signal to London '*peccavi*', being the Latin for 'I have sinned'.

To the right is *William Behnes'* 1861 bronze of **Major-General Sir Henry Havelock [20]**, famed for his part in the reliefs of Cawnpore and Lucknow during the Indian Mutiny. Havelock died at Lucknow and was awarded a posthumous baronetcy. His statue is said to be the first to have been created from a photograph.

There are two higher-level plinths at the back of the square. To the right, in the corner, is *Francis Chantrey's* **George IV [21]**, first commissioned in 1829 for the top of **Marble Arch** in its original location in front of Buckingham Palace, but only cast in 1836 and erected (after Marble Arch was relocated) in 1843. Like *Chantrey's* near contemporary equestrian statue of the **Duke of Wellington** in front of the Royal Exchange, this is an austere, hatless and stirrupless, classical work, uncharacteristic, one might think, of one of England's more self-indulgent monarchs, even if invariably topped by one or more of the myriad pigeons of the square.

The left-hand plinth is '**the empty plinth**' **[22]**, which gives rise to more controversy and hot air than any erected statue in London. Should its monumental tenant be old or bold, classical or avant-garde, dead or alive? And so on. In recent years it has been the short-lived home for a succession of manifestly inappropriate modernist works, all completely out of keeping with the grandeur of the square, and usually the initiative of some mischievous populist politician.

It would be an ideal home for a statue of Queen Elizabeth II but for the moment it remains 'the empty plinth'.

Briefly leave the square on its west side and walk down Cockspur Street to the small triangle at the junction with Pall Mall. You are now standing behind Canada House. You will see *Matthew Cotes Wyatt's* 1836 equestrian statue of **George III [23]**. (You can see another earlier work of a younger George III at Somerset House, see page 83.) Walk around the junction and into Pall Mall and back into the square.

In front of the west side of the National Gallery stands a very classical **James II [24]**. Like his father and elder brother, James became a public statue in his own lifetime, and this bronze of 1685 was probably another piece by *Arnold Quellin* in the studio of *Grinling Gibbons*. Apart from the unusual costume, the statue is also interesting as being one of central London's most moved public monuments. First erected in the Privy Gardens in Whitehall in 1685, it was re-erected in front of Gwydyr House in 1897, then in St James's Park in 1903, before coming to the National Gallery in 1948. It also spent some time in a box in the garden of Gwydyr House and much of the Second World War in Aldwych Underground Station.

Moving to the east frontage of the National Gallery, there is an exact life-size bronze of **George Washington [25]**, at 1.87 metres (6 feet 2 inches) in height. It is a bronze replica of the original eighteenth-century marble by *Jean Antoine Houdon* in the State Capitol at Richmond, Virginia, presented to the nation by the Commonwealth of Virginia in 1921.

Naval Commemoration

But this is, above all, the Royal Navy's square. It is dominated, of course, by one monument – **Nelson [26]**, England's most famous and successful admiral, the victor of Trafalgar in 1805. It is a 5.2-metre (17-foot) tall statue in Craigleith stone by *Edward Hodges Baily* on a 51-metre (167-foot) tall Devon-granite column designed by *William Railton,* all of 1843. The bronze reliefs on the four sides of the base of the column came some ten years later and depict Nelson's principal triumphs: on the east side, Copenhagen, by *John Ternouth*; on the south, the Death of Nelson at Trafalgar, by *John Carew*; on the west, St Vincent, by *M. L. Watson* and *W. F. Woodington*; and on the north, the Nile, also by *Woodington.* The famous four lions are later still, of 1867, designed by *Edwin Landseer* and cast by *Carlo Marochetti.* The entire composition is one of those quintessential London icons, like '**Eros**'and **Churchill**, which simply speaks for itself and is now beyond any sort of aesthetic criticism.

The square itself is a nineteenth-century creation whose principal architects were *John Nash* and *Charles Barry*, and which replaced the Royal Mews of several hundred years' standing. The quatrefoil fountain basins are the work of *Barry,* their central fountains (by *Edwin Lutyens*) and the outer mermen (*Charles Wheeler*) and inner mermaids (*William McMillan*) being twentieth-century additions in honour of Admirals of the Fleet Earl Jellicoe and Earl Beatty. At the back of the main floor of the square, now set to the right-hand side since the creation of the central steps leading up to the National Gallery, are three busts of Admirals of the Fleet: **Jellicoe [27]**, **Beatty [28]** and **Cunningham [29]**. **Jellicoe** is by *Charles Wheeler* and **Beatty** by *William McMillan*, both in 1948, and **Cunningham** by *Franta Belsky* in 1967. Jellicoe commanded the Grand Fleet at Jutland in 1916 and was, in Churchill's words, 'The only man on either side who could lose the war in an afternoon'; Beatty, Jellicoe's successor, was the youngest (at only thirty-eight) and most glamorous admiral since Nelson, an Admiral of the Fleet at forty-eight, and for seven and a half years after the Great War the longest-serving First Sea Lord, or professional head of the Royal Navy; Cunningham, the third of the trio, was far and away the pre-eminent British admiral of the Second World War.

You need to look down rather than up, just for a change, in order to see the – in every sense – footnote to this walk. Set into the paving slabs of the square, on the north side of the main lower level, are cast bronze measures of the imperial standards of length. Placed here by the Standards Department of the Board of Trade in 1876, and stated to be accurate at 62° Fahrenheit, are the official records of an inch, a foot and a yard; of a hundred feet; and of those splendidly un-metric measures, the pole, the perch and the chain with all its links.

There is an entrance to Charing Cross Road Underground Station at the south-east corner of the square.

6. THE WEST END – FROM PARK CRESCENT TO THE ROYAL ACADEMY

START	Regent's Park Underground Station (Bakerloo line)
FINISH	Piccadilly Circus Underground Station (Piccadilly and Bakerloo lines)
DISTANCE	4.75 km (3 miles)
DURATION	1 ½ hours

A President and a Duke on the Crescent

When you emerge from Regent's Park Underground Station's only exit, you find yourself in the sculpturally unpromising environment of the Marylebone Road, the main east-west arterial traffic route through central London. But a few yards' walk either way brings you to one or other end of Park Crescent, one of *John Nash's* masterpieces round the lower half of Regent's Park, with its near-pristine elegantly stuccoed facades that were restored in the early 1960s.

You are going to go to the east, so turn right out of the tube. At the east end of the crescent, just beyond it and facing on to Marylebone Road, is a bronze bust of **John F. Kennedy [1]**, thirty-fifth President of the United States. It is the work of the American sculptor *Jacques Lipchitz* and it was unveiled by the President's brother, Senator Robert Kennedy, on 15 May 1965. It is a copy of the bust in the Library of Congress in Washington DC. The bust itself is not a wonderful likeness and is principally interesting because its cost (as the plinth records) was met by subscriptions from over fifty thousand readers of the *Sunday Telegraph*, all barred from contributing more than £1 each (and most, one imagines, having given a very great deal less than that).

Walk around the crescent and the first full statue on this walk stands in the crescent's garden, facing down Portland Place. It is an 1825 bronze of the then **Duke of Kent [2]**, the fourth son of George III, by *Sebastian Gahagan*. Although the duke had early military pretensions and was in later life greatly involved in charitable works – in his left hand he holds a scroll marked 'Annual Report' – he is perhaps best known for being the father of Queen Victoria, whose birth he survived by barely eight months. Victoria was born on 24 May 1819 and the duke died on 23 January 1820.

Portland Place

Cross into Portland Place. This was the 1770s creation of the *Adam* brothers, Robert and James, and in its day was one of the widest and most elegant streets in London. Only Georgian Bloomsbury has the same sense of gracious spaciousness about it and few other London streets have a central reservation – a considerable boon, it appears, to subsequent generations of sculptors. Start walking down the street, on its west side.

This is also 'medical' London (Harley Street is only one block to the west), and the first sculpture that you will see is a bronze bust of **Lister** [3], by *Thomas Brock* in 1922. Joseph Lister was the 'father of antiseptic surgery', and it has been said of him that: 'It is probable that no man's work has had a greater influence on the progress of surgery; the saving of human life and suffering that he effected is incalculable.' (ODNB) He lived latterly in Park Crescent, became the first medical peer and was one of the twelve original members of the Order of Merit, when it was established by Edward VII in 1902.

Next down Portland Place is obviously a soldier, but the uniform is unfamiliar, topped by a diamond-shaped kepi. His plain four-square stance is slightly reminiscent of the two airmen standing outside St Clement Danes (see page 84), and indeed all three statues are by *Faith Winter*, this being the most recent, in 2000. He is **General Sikorski** [4], head of the Polish government in exile and commander of the Polish Armed Forces from 1939 until his death in an air crash in 1943. He stands between the Chinese Embassy (Numbers 49–51) on the west side and the Royal Institute of British Architects (Number 66) on the east, and looks sternly at the Polish Embassy (Number 47), one building on from the Chinese Embassy on the south side of the Weymouth Street junction.

This walk does not go into the **Royal Institute of British Architects (RIBA)** [5], on the east side of the street, but you can admire *George Grey Wornum's* remarkable exterior design – 'A timeless exemplar of the call in the RIBA's charter for the advancement and promotion of architecture', as Paul Hyett, a past President of the RIBA has described it – and the sculptures on the Portland Place facade (all dating from the construction of the building in 1934). The relief figure of '**Architectural Aspiration**' over the giant central window is by *Edward Bainbridge Copnall* and the figures of **Man and Woman** by *James Woodford* on the free-standing columns either side of the entrance. The cast bronze doors were also by *Woodford*, each one being 3.6 metres (12 feet) by 1.8 metres (6 feet) and weighing 1¹/₂ tons, and showing in deep relief '**London's river and its buildings**'.

The Polish Embassy was, in an earlier incarnation, the home of Field Marshal Earl Roberts (see page 43) and it is therefore not inappropriate (although coincidental) that another 'Indian' field marshal should have his statue here, outside the embassy. This is a 1922 bronze by *John Tweed* of **Field Marshal Sir George White** [6], who succeeded Roberts as Commander-in-Chief of the Indian Army in 1893, achieved subsequent fame (or notoriety) at the Siege of Ladysmith in 1899–1900 at the outbreak of the Boer War and was later Governor of Gibraltar and then of the Royal Hospital at Chelsea, before his death in 1912. The statue was commissioned and executed without difficulties, but the hospital commissioners refused to have it at Chelsea, either at the hospital itself or in Royal Avenue, and it ended up in Portland Place.

All the central statues and busts that you have met in Portland Place face south, and the next is no exception. **Quintin Hogg** [7] (1845–1903) was a successful Victorian businessman and an early football enthusiast (not to be confused with his grandson of the same name, the twentieth-century politician and Lord Chancellor). His main concern, however, was philanthropy. It is as the founder of the Regent Street Polytechnic, and thereby the transformer of 'further education' in London, that he is principally remembered. His bronze is by *George*

Frampton (better known as the sculptor of **Peter Pan** in Kensington Gardens, see page 20), in 1906. He sits reading a book, flanked by two obvious schoolboys, one carrying a football. On one side of the plinth is a touching tribute to his wife Alice, 'whose unfailing love and devotion contributed so greatly to the success of the Polytechnic', and on the other a memorial to the war dead of the polytechnic, in both world wars.

Continuing down Portland Place, you then come to one of what Pevsner describes as 'the two ugly ducklings' of Portland Place: the BBC's **Broadcasting House [8]** on the east side of the street and the Langham Hotel, more or less directly opposite on the west side. Note the exterior sculpture by *Eric Gill* and in particular the figure of Ariel over the main entrance of Broadcasting House off Langham Place.

Right next to BBC Broadcasting House is All Souls, Langham Place church. In the exterior colonnade of the church is a 1956 bust of its architect, **John Nash [9]**, by *Cecil Thomas*, after the original 1831 bust by *William Behnes*. The church – consecrated on 25 November 1824 – is an appropriate place for Nash to be commemorated because it completed his scheme for Regent Street and Portland Place, with Langham Place as the neat S-bend link between those two great thoroughfares. Described by Pevsner as the greatest piece of town planning London has ever seen, Nash's route connected Carlton House in St James's to Regent's Park. Of the works undertaken to implement Nash's design, executed over a twenty-five year period from 1811, few buildings survive between Park Crescent and Carlton House Terrace, but the route of Regent Street remains entirely as Nash laid it out, and as his bust surveys it today.

Cavendish Square

Cross over the road and turn right into Cavendish Place. Continue walking and you will come to Cavendish Square. This was first laid out as a square in 1717 by *John Prince*, who is commemorated by the street bearing his name just off the south-east corner of the square, even if the buildings around the square were not substantially completed for another fifty years. It was the centrepiece of the new Marylebone Estate of Edward Harley, Earl of Oxford and Mortimer, and was named after his wife, Lady Henrietta Cavendish Holles (all of her names are street names in the immediate vicinity). In an eclectic collection of buildings round the square, the post-war reconstruction of the John Lewis department store is probably now the best known. The square conceals one of central London's larger underground car parks.

Halfway along the north side of the square you will find four Palladian houses, Numbers 11–14, built by George Foster Tufnell around 1769. Numbers 11–13 were owned (and occupied) by the Sisters of the Society of the Holy Child Jesus at the time of their extensive damage during the Second World War. The society commissioned the then young architect and goldsmith *Louis Osman* to oversee the restoration of the buildings after the war. *Osman's* plans laid particular importance on the new bridge over Dean's Mews, which now connects Numbers 12 and 13, but he was adamant in his dealings with the society that the bridge would be ridiculous without a sculpture. He overcame the considerable reluctance of the Sisters and secured the participation of *Jacob Epstein*, who told *Osman* that he had 'never had such a wonderful proposal'. *Epstein* accepted merely a nominal fee and went on to produce what is probably his finest public work in London, the **Virgin and Child [10]** (see illustration, right), on the bridge. The sculpture conveys both stillness and great sorrow. It was cast in lead partly because *Osman* was anxious to avoid any green stain on his Portland stone and partly for economy: the 3 tons of lead largely came from the roof and downpipes of the reconstructed buildings. It was unveiled on Ascension Thursday (15 May) 1953 by Richard Austen 'Rab' Butler, then the Chancellor of the Exchequer.

In the middle of the square is an empty plinth (but a less contentious one than its counterpart in Trafalgar Square, see page 62). Its inscription records that it previously supported an equestrian statue of **William Duke of Cumberland**, third son of George II, best known perhaps for his suppression of the Jacobean Rebellion of 1745 and consequently remembered more fondly in England than in Scotland. The statue was erected in 1770 at the instigation of Lieutenant-General William Strode, but was removed by the 5th Duke of Portland in 1868 and melted down. The plinth has been untenanted ever since and the only statue in the square is that of **Lord George [Cavendish] Bentinck [11]**, a bronze by *Thomas Campbell* in 1851, on the south side of the square opposite Holles Street. A younger son of the 4th Duke and a nephew of George Canning, Lord George was a man of many parts: soldier, sportsman, Member of Parliament, protectionist politician (and one of the principal architects of the fall of Sir Robert Peel's government in 1846). He was perhaps best known, and loved, for being a champion of the turf.

Either Side of Oxford Street

Leave Cavendish Square on its south side and walk down the east side of Holles Street. At the corner of Holles Street and Oxford Street, occupying the otherwise blank corner facade of John Lewis, is a work by *Barbara Hepworth*. '**Winged Figure**' [12], of 1963, is a large but surprisingly (or perhaps, consequently) bland piece, in stringed aluminium. Despite its prominent location it probably goes unnoticed by virtually all the shoppers who scurry underneath it. On the other hand, it is a lasting tribute to the artistic patronage and good taste of the directors of John Lewis.

Brave the retailing multitude and cross Oxford Street into Hanover Place. You are now in Mayfair and heading towards Hanover Square, first laid out in 1713, only four years before Cavendish

Square. As in Cavendish Square, very few buildings survive from those early years and nowadays Hanover Square is best known as the home of several distinguished firms of estate agents and surveyors, although the nineteenth-century French statesman Prince Talleyrand probably has a fair claim to have been the square's most distinguished resident of all time. But you are here in order to see one statue – *Francis Chantrey's* 1831 bronze of **William Pitt the Younger [13]**, best seen by walking round the outside of the square and standing on the traffic island at the top of St George Street. **Pitt** stands on a granite plinth on the south side of the central gardens, facing down St George Street, in contemporary dress but wearing a rather academically classical cloak. He was Prime Minister from the extraordinary age of twenty-four until his death in office in 1806 at the age of forty-six, with only one brief (and largely voluntary) break between 1801 and 1804. Subscriptions for his statue were first raised on his resignation in 1801, but were shelved upon his resuming office three years later: Pitt himself made it clear that he would prefer a posthumous monument. After his death, statues in Glasgow and Cambridge and the monument inside the Guildhall all preceded *Chantrey's* statue, which was eventually erected (not without contention) in the general political turbulence immediately preceding the Great Reform Act of 1832.

Leave Hanover Square at the south-west corner and walk westwards along the south side of Brook Street toward Grosvenor Square. Just the other side of Bond Street, Numbers 23 and 25 Brook Street sport two of the blue plaques that abound on central London buildings, recording the names of the great and the good who have shed their lustre on particular buildings. This duo records the delightfully implausible pairing of George Frederick Handel, who has a good claim to being called England's greatest composer and who was an early tenant of Number 25, and Jimi Hendrix, the 1960s rock star, who was a much briefer tenant of Number 23 over two hundred years later. The upper floors of both houses have since been combined to form the Handel House Museum, which makes a very worthwhile diversion.

Grosvenor Square

Continue walking and you will come to Grosvenor Square. It is the largest square in Mayfair, first begun in the 1720s, and it could be called the centre of American London, with the huge late 1950s embassy building, designed by the Finnish-born American *Eero Saarinen*, occupying the whole of the west side. In the square itself are two of London's four full-size statues of American presidents: in the middle of the north side of the gardens, **Roosevelt [14]**, 'FDR'; and in the north-west corner, just outside the embassy, **Eisenhower [15]**, 'Ike'.

Roosevelt is a bronze by *William Reid Dick*, and was unveiled by Mrs Roosevelt on 12 April 1948, the third anniversary of FDR's death. The statue has two particular points of interest: at Mrs Roosevelt's insistence, FDR was depicted standing (albeit with a stick), even though he is generally remembered in his polio-stricken seated position; and the very considerable cost of the statue (over £40,000 in the money of the time) was entirely met by British public subscription. The walls of the two flanking basins record FDR's famous four 'freedoms', of worship and speech, and from want and fear.

Eisenhower, on the other hand, is 'all American', a bronze by an American sculptor *Robert Dean* and presented by the City of Kansas in 1989. The posture – hands firmly on hips, the determined gaze – is very reminiscent of countless wartime photos of Ike. At the time of writing, it seems likely that **FDR** and **Ike** will soon be joined by a new statue of Ronald Reagan, the fortieth US President.

Return to the gardens in the centre of the square. On the south side, facing **FDR**, is the **Monument to the Eagle Squadrons [16]** – the three RAF 'Eagle' squadrons that were largely composed of American volunteers fighting for Britain before the US joined the war at the end of 1941. The monument, which was completed in 1986, is topped by a cadet-sized bronze eagle by *Elisabeth Frink*, and the 244 American and 16 British pilots are named on the pedestal of the monument. On the east side, opposite the Italian Embassy, is the **September 11 Memorial Garden [17]**. This small, discrete formal garden was officially opened on 11 September 2003 in memory of all those who lost their lives in the 9/11 terrorist attacks on the USA.

Between the Square and Piccadilly

Leave Grosvenor Square by its south-east corner and cross the road into Carlos Place and walk down the west side. You passed Claridge's Hotel in Brook Street and now here is the Connaught Hotel (you will see Brown's Hotel in Albemarle Street and the Ritz on Piccadilly before you end the walk), just before you hit Mount Street. On the triangle outside the Connaught Hotel is a bronze **female nude [18]** at her ablutions, which also doubles up as a fountain (once again, dormant). She is by *Emilio Greco* in 1973 and was presented to the City of Westminster in 1987 by the then President of Italy.

Cross over Mount Street and turn left and walk eastwards along this street until you reach Berkeley Square. Berkeley Square is famous for its singing nightingale and enormous plane trees, and is surprisingly bereft of any sculpture apart from the statuesque fountain at the far south end. A lead equestrian statue of George III by the French sculptor Beaupré was erected in 1772 in the middle of the square, but was removed in 1827 on account of its disrepair and replaced by the existing pump house or gazebo. Variously described as an anonymous nymph and the **Woman of Samaria [19]**, the fountain is a white Carrara-marble figure of a classically unclad woman holding an overflowing vase as a fountain. She is the work of *Alexander Munro* in 1858 and was given to the square by the 3rd Marquess of Lansdowne (Lansdowne House, then one of the grand houses of London and now the Lansdowne Club, is just off the south-west corner of the square, in Curzon Street). She was restored in 1994 and reoriented so as to face south.

From the romantic to the outright kitsch. Leave the square on the east side and walk along the south side of Bruton Street, doffing your hat to Number 17 where Queen Elizabeth II was born (the actual house having long since been demolished). Turn right into New Bond Street and walk to the pedestrianized intersection of New Bond and Old Bond streets. You will see the 1995 work of *Lawrence Holofcener*, '**Allies' [20]**. This comprises two sub-life size bronzes of Churchill and FDR sitting on a bench. As a tourist attraction, it has been a huge success, the sculptor having thoughtfully left a space between the two bronzes in which one tourist can sit while being photographed by his or her companion. Resemblance to either original subject matter, however, is poor, and there is not a glimmer of the grandeur which is captured and portrayed by either *Reid Dick's* **FDR** (see above) or *Roberts-Jones'* **Churchill** (see page 50).

Turn right into Grafton Street and left again into Albemarle Street, past Brown's Hotel. Continue walking until you reach Stafford Street. Turn right on to Stafford Street and walk in

this direction until you come to Dover Street. Turn left on to Dover Street and continue walking, which will bring you to another work by *Elisabeth Frink*, '**Horse and Rider**' [21] (see illustration, above) of 1975, at the bottom of Dover Street. (There is another cast of this work at the top of the High Street in Winchester.) Cross over Piccadilly, and you will see the Ritz to your right. Walk a short way down the west side of St James's, then turn left into Jermyn Street. '**Beau' Brummell** [22], the quintessential Regency dandy, stands at the bottom of the Piccadilly Arcade. Jermyn Street is associated with classic male fashion, so this 2002 life-size bronze by *Irena Sedlecka* is therefore most appropriately situated.

Royal Academy of Arts

Walk through the Piccadilly Arcade and cross to the north side of Piccadilly. Turn to your right and walk very briefly in the direction of Piccadilly Circus and you will soon be at Burlington House, the home of the Royal Academy of Arts (RA). The Academy was founded in 1768 by George III, arguably the greatest of all British royal patrons of the arts. (See page 82 for an earlier home of the RA, in Somerset House on the Strand.) This walk only takes in the courtyard of Burlington House, and the statues in and around it. As you pass through the west side of the gateway off Piccadilly, take a look at the prototype 'K2' public telephone box of 1926, designed by *Giles Gilbert Scott*. It was made of timber rather than the standard production in cast iron and

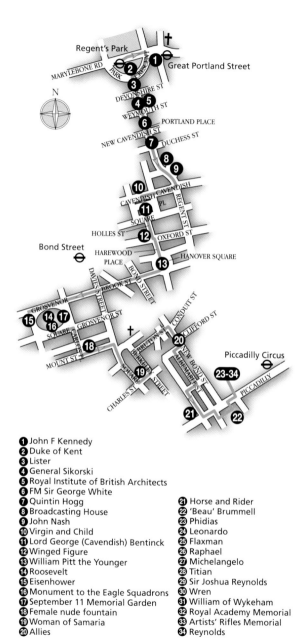

1 John F Kennedy
2 Duke of Kent
3 Lister
4 General Sikorski
5 Royal Institute of British Architects
6 FM Sir George White
7 Quintin Hogg
8 Broadcasting House
9 John Nash
10 Virgin and Child
11 Lord George (Cavendish) Bentinck
12 Winged Figure
13 William Pitt the Younger
14 Roosevelt
15 Eisenhower
16 Monument to the Eagle Squadrons
17 September 11 Memorial Garden
18 Female nude fountain
19 Woman of Samaria
20 Allies

21 Horse and Rider
22 'Beau' Brummell
23 Phidias
24 Leonardo
25 Flaxman
26 Raphael
27 Michelangelo
28 Titian
29 Sir Joshua Reynolds
30 Wren
31 William of Wykeham
32 Royal Academy Memorial
33 Artists' Rifles Memorial
34 Reynolds

is now proudly labelled as a listed (i.e. protected) building.

At second-floor level, on the facade of Burlington House itself which faces you as you enter the courtyard, the 1870s conversion of the building to its present use as the RA – a conversion described by Pevsner as an act of 'High Victorian cruelty' – included an eclectic row of statues, whose common thread is not immediately obvious. From left to right they are: **Phidias [23]** (said to be the greatest of the Ancient Greek sculptors) by *Joseph Durham*; **Leonardo [24]** by *Edward Stephens*; **Flaxman [25]** (the English sculptor, whose career spanned over half a century before his death in 1826) and **Raphael [26]**, both by *Henry Weekes;* **Michelangelo [27]** and **Titian [28]**, both by *William Calder Marshall*; **Sir Joshua Reynolds [29]**, the first President of the RA; and **Wren [30]**, both again by *Stephens,* and lastly and perplexingly **William of Wykeham [31]** (medieval Bishop of Winchester, Chancellor of England, and founder of New College, Oxford and Winchester College, a man of many accomplishments, but not himself an artist), again by *Durham*. Below them, at either end of the ground-level arcade, are two modest but moving war memorials – the **Royal Academy Memorial [32]** to the west, designed by *Trenwith Wills*, and the **Artists' Rifles Memorial [33]**, designed by *Geoffrey Webb*, to the east.

In the middle of the courtyard is a second and more conspicuous statue of **Reynolds [34]** (see illustration, above), a bronze by *Alfred Drury* in 1931. Besides being the leading portrait painter of his day, Reynolds could claim England's leading man of letters, Dr Johnson, as his greatest friend. Drury's statue vividly conveys the dynamic energy for which Reynolds was well known. The plinth was designed by *Giles Gilbert Scott*.

Once you have viewed the works in the courtyard, go back to the gateway, turn left and walk up Piccadilly to Piccadilly Circus. There are many entrances to Piccadilly Circus Underground Station around the Circus.

7. THE EMBANKMENT – FROM WESTMINSTER TO BLACKFRIARS

START	Westminster Underground Station (Jubilee, Circle and District lines)
FINISH	Mansion House Underground Station (Circle and District lines)
DISTANCE	3 km (1 ³/₄ miles)
DURATION	1 hour

This walk follows the Embankment downstream between Westminster and Blackfriars bridges. Save for a brief sally over to the South Bank at the start, you will stay on the north side. Although the huge bend in the river means that the journey between these two bridges is much shorter on the South Bank, the north side has far more statues and monuments.

Leave Westminster Underground Station via the Embankment exit. You will emerge immediately downstream of Westminster Bridge and almost underneath a fearsome scythe-wheeled chariot, driven by **Boadicea [1]** (see illustration, below), Queen of the Iceni, accompanied by her two scantily clad daughters. The tribe of the Iceni in East Anglia rose in revolt against the Romans in 61 AD, but the revolt was savagely suppressed. Boadicea took poison rather than surrender. She was a very British heroine, ideally suited to Victorian monumental sculpture. The

entire group is a *Thornycroft* family affair, and a protracted one at that: *Thomas Thornycroft* began the work in 1856; his two daughters modelled for Boadicea's daughters; the work first appeared in plaster in 1871; *Thomas* died in 1885, having lost interest in the work; it was completed and cast in bronze by his second son, *Hamo*, who was also responsible for the horses. *Thomas's* elder son *John*, the distinguished naval architect (designer of the Royal Navy's first torpedo boats and destroyers, and founder of the shipbuilders later known as Vosper Thornycroft), presented the work to the then newly established London County Council in 1902. The *Thornycrofts'* original expectation was that the work would be erected on Parliament Hill in Highgate, which was said to be Boadicea's burial site. Hyde Park Corner was another possibility but in the end the chosen site was here, on Westminster Bridge. On the plinth are the lines from the eighteenth-century poet William Cowper's 'Boadicea': 'Regions Caesar never knew / Thy posterity shall sway'.

A Brief Visit to the South Bank

As you cross the bridge, think of Wordsworth's lines from 'Composed upon Westminster Bridge' (1807): 'Earth has not anything to show more fair' (even if he might have thought the view of central London today even more spectacular from the higher vantage point of Waterloo Bridge). At the other end of the bridge you can see the **South Bank Lion [2]** (see illustration, above). The **South Bank Lion** is the work of *W. F. Woodington* in 1837. It is a very late example of the use of Coade stone – a very durable, composite, reconstituted stone invented by its eponymous founder in the late eighteenth century. This was the largest of three lions that stood outside or on top of the old Red Lion Brewery at Waterloo Bridge. The brewery was demolished, after war damage, to make way for the Festival of Britain and in particular the Festival Hall. This lion was preserved at the express request of George VI, and after a brief stay at Waterloo Station found its way here.

Military Memorials

Retrace your steps back to **Boadicea** and follow the Victoria Embankment, walking along the side closest to the river. Almost immediately you come to the most recent monument included in this walk, the 2005 **Battle of Britain Memorial [3]**, the work of *Paul Day*. The 'Battle of Britain' is the collective name given to the air battles between the Royal Air Force and the German Luftwaffe that took place over south-east England between 10 July and 31 October 1940. A critical point of those battles was on 15 September, now commemorated as Battle of Britain Day, when two major Luftwaffe attacks were repulsed by the RAF, with heavy German losses. The Luftwaffe's failure saved Britain from defeat, invasion and conquest, and ultimately cost Germany the war. Essentially two long, low walls, decorated in prominent relief with scenes representing aspects of the battle, the main purpose of the memorial is to record the names of 'The Few' – the 2,936 pilots from Britain, the Commonwealth, the United States, Poland and beyond, who flew and fought in the battle (544 of whom died in the battle, while another 795 did not survive the war). They earned the glorious and immortal tribute of Churchill in the House of Commons on 20 August 1940: 'Never in the field of human conflict was so much owed by so many to so few.'

There are more 'air' memorials immediately ahead: the Ministry of Defence, just beyond the green on the other side of the road, started life as the Air Ministry, and the airmen have bagged this pitch. Continue walking and a short distance from the **Battle of Britain Memorial** is the **RAF Memorial [4]** of 1923, designed by *Reginald Blomfield* and topped by a gilt-bronze eagle by *William Reid Dick*. Among *Blomfield's* better known memorial works are the Menin Gate in Ypres and the Cross of Sacrifice in every British war cemetery. Viewing the eagle from the green opposite – or perhaps searching the skies for his returning bombers – is *Oscar Nemon's* 1975 bronze of **Marshal of the RAF Viscount Portal [5]**, a roughly finished piece apart from the head. Portal was the Chief of the Air Staff during most of the Second World War.

At some distance from **Portal** and back towards Westminster, on the same green in front of the Ministry of Defence, stands *William McMillan's* 1961 bronze of the founder of the independent Royal Air Force and its first chief of staff throughout the 1920s, **Marshal of the RAF Viscount Trenchard [6]**, whose subsequent career included a spell as the commissioner of Metropolitan Police.

Behind **Portal** is *James Butler's* **Fleet Air Arm Memorial [7]** of 2000 – part Daedalus, the wiser father of rasher Icarus, part wartime airman. At the extreme Westminster end of this row is the **Chindit Monument [8]**, by *Frank Forster* in 1990. This is a memorial to the heroism of the 'Chindit' forces who fought behind the Japanese lines in Burma. At the other end is **Gordon [9]** – Major-General Sir Charles Gordon, "Chinese" Gordon, soldier and mystic, killed by the forces of the Mahdi at Khartoum in 1885, thus earning his place in the pantheon of Victorian immortals. *Hamo Thornycroft's* 1888 bronze spent the first half of its life in Trafalgar Square; it departed for Mentmore during the Second World War and came to its present site in 1953. It is said to be a good likeness of Gordon, even if it does also remarkably resemble Charlton Heston, whose many film roles included Gordon.

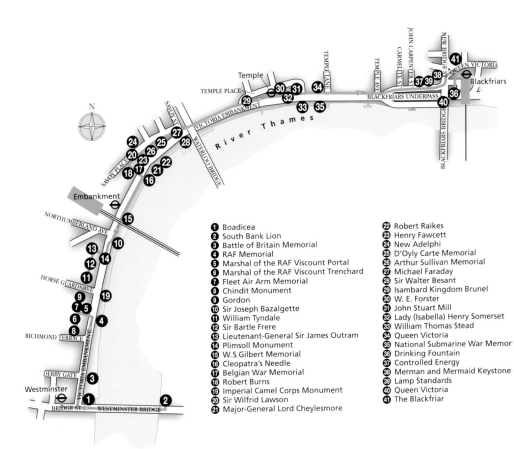

Temple
TEMPLE PLACE
Blackfriars
BLACKFRIARS UNDERPASS

River Thames

Embankment

Westminster

- ❶ Boadicea
- ❷ South Bank Lion
- ❸ Battle of Britain Memorial
- ❹ RAF Memorial
- ❺ Marshal of the RAF Viscount Portal
- ❻ Marshal of the RAF Viscount Trenchard
- ❼ Fleet Air Arm Memorial
- ❽ Chindit Monument
- ❾ Gordon
- ❿ Sir Joseph Bazalgette
- ⓫ William Tyndale
- ⓬ Sir Bartle Frere
- ⓭ Lieutenant-General Sir James Outram
- ⓮ Plimsoll Monument
- ⓯ W.S. Gilbert Memorial
- ⓰ Cleopatra's Needle
- ⓱ Belgian War Memorial
- ⓲ Robert Burns
- ⓳ Imperial Camel Corps Monument
- ⓴ Sir Wilfrid Lawson
- ㉑ Major-General Lord Cheylesmore

- ㉒ Robert Raikes
- ㉓ Henry Fawcett
- ㉔ New Adelphi
- ㉕ D'Oyly Carte Memorial
- ㉖ Arthur Sullivan Memorial
- ㉗ Michael Faraday
- ㉘ Sir Walter Besant
- ㉙ Isambard Kingdom Brunel
- ㉚ W. E. Forster
- ㉛ John Stuart Mill
- ㉜ Lady (Isabella) Henry Somerset
- ㉝ William Thomas Stead
- ㉞ Queen Victoria
- ㉟ National Submarine War Memor
- ㊱ Drinking Fountain
- ㊲ Controlled Energy
- ㊳ Merman and Mermaid Keystone
- ㊴ Lamp Standards
- ㊵ Queen Victoria
- ㊶ The Blackfriar

Visible History of the Embankment

The Thames has not always been bordered by neat embankments, and this relatively short walk has three surviving indicators of how much wider the river was before the embankments were constructed. Behind **Gordon**, just in front of the Ministry of Defence, you can see the remains of Queen Mary's Steps, the water entrance to the old Palace of Whitehall in the seventeenth century. You will see the next two examples later in the walk: in the main Embankment Gardens to the north of Hungerford Railway Bridge, York Water Gate – the early seventeenth-century water entrance to the Duke of Buckingham's mansion, at what is now the bottom of Buckingham Street – is a good 90 metres (98 yards) from the present riverbank, some 15 hectares (37 acres) having been reclaimed in the construction of the Embankment and the gardens; the river entrance to Somerset House, on the north side of Waterloo Bridge, is now a dual carriageway's width from the river.

The principal credit for the central London embankment works that you see today and for much of London's sewerage system, goes to a remarkable Victorian engineer, **Sir Joseph Bazalgette [10]**, whose bronze portrait bust monument of 1901 by *G. B. Simonds* is mounted on the Embankment wall at the bottom of Northumberland Avenue, immediately upstream of the railway bridge. The state of the river and London's sewage grew progressively worse during the nineteenth century, but it was the 'Great Stink' of 1858 – the smell during that hot summer was so bad that Parliament had to rise – that compelled the urgent transformation of the 1860s, to the present embankments and sewerage. **Bazalgette's** memorial bears the apt subscription *'flumini vincula posuit'* – 'he put chains to the river'.

Embankment Gardens Between Two Avenues

Before you reach the railway bridge, in the section of the Embankment Gardens between Horse Guards Avenue and Northumberland Avenue, there are three more large Victorian bronzes, by eminent sculptors whose names appear many times in these walks: **William Tyndale [11]** by *Edgar Boehm* in 1884, **Sir Bartle Frere [12]** by *Thomas Brock* in 1888 and **Lieutenant-General Sir James Outram [13]** by *Matthew Noble* in 1871. They stand in front of those high twin monstrosities, Whitehall Court and the National Liberal Club.

Tyndale was the first translator of the Bible into English from Greek, nearly half a millennium ago, and was martyred for his pains in Belgium in 1536; the Authorized Version of King James is substantially based on Tyndale's work. Frere was a distinguished Victorian colonial governor. Outram was another of those larger-than-life Victorian soldiers, best known for his defence of Lucknow during the Indian Mutiny after its first relief by Havelock (see page 61) and until its final relief by Campbell (later Lord Clyde, see page 39). Of Outram it was said that 'a fox is a fool and a lion a coward compared with James Outram', and he was toasted by his military senior, Charles Napier, at a dinner in 1842 as 'the Bayard of India, *sans peur* and *sans reproche*'; indeed, his gravestone in Westminster Abbey bears the legend 'The Bayard of India'.

Just before you leave this section of the gardens, in its own small enclosure, fronting on to the Embankment rather than in the gardens, is the **Plimsoll Monument [14]** by *F. V. Blundstone* in 1929. You will see it, therefore, by returning to the Embankment. It commemorates Samuel Plimsoll, the Victorian politician whose agitation in the 1870s led to the Merchant Shipping Act 1876, requiring the marking on a ship's side showing the limit of legal submersion under various conditions, the marking having subsequently taken Plimsoll's name. This put an end to the practice of sending to sea overloaded and heavily insured old ships whose owners pocketed huge profits when the ships sank. The monument was 'erected by the members of the National Union of Seamen in grateful recognition of his services to the men of the sea of all nations'. **Plimsoll** himself is merely a bust, but he is evidently grievously lamented by supporting bronze statues of a sailor and a semi-clad woman with wreathes. *Blundstone* himself is better known as the principal sculptor of the Memorial to the Missing at Tyne Cot, just east of Ypres, the largest British war cemetery in the world.

Between Hungerford Bridge and Embankment Gardens

On the river wall immediately downstream of the railway bridge is *George Frampton's* 1915 **W. S. Gilbert Memorial [15]**, a portrait bronze with accompanying figures of tragedy and comedy. Gilbert is as inextricably linked to Sullivan (whose own monument you shall meet within a few yards) as other great pairings in the spheres of music and entertainment like Laurel and Hardy, or Flanders and Swann, and their respective monuments are here because the operettas that are their most enduring memorial were first staged at the Savoy Theatre, just off the Strand.

Continue walking along the embankment and you will come to **Cleopatra's Needle [16]** – a hieroglyphically adorned Egyptian obelisk, now about 3,500 years old. Originally erected at Heliopolis (pretty much modern-day Cairo) and moved to Alexandria by the Emperor Augustus, this obelisk and its twin were given to Britain and the United States in the nineteenth century. The London sibling, although gifted in 1819, was only transported to Britain in 1877, in a purpose-built iron cylinder that broke loose during a storm in the Bay of Biscay.

On the other side of the Embankment roadway is *Reginald Blomfield's* 1920 **Belgian War Memorial [17]**, 'From the grateful people of Belgium'. Cross the road to view it, and then return a few yards in an upstream direction, to the entrance to this section of Embankment Gardens.

Embankment Gardens

In the gardens themselves a mixed bag of statuary stands between the large open green at the upstream end and Waterloo Bridge. **Robert Burns [18]**, perhaps the world's most commemorated poet after England's own Bard, is an 1884 bronze by *John Steell*. The military world is represented by *Cecil Brown's* 1920 **Imperial Camel Corps Monument [19]**, a delightful small-size bronze of a camel and rider on a small square plinth, recording the names of all the Camel Corps' units and engagements during the Great War. **Sir Wilfrid Lawson [20]**, Member of Parliament and wit, a prominent temperance promoter, is a 1909 bronze by *David McGill*, commissioned by the Temperance Society and unveiled by the Prime Minister of the day, H. H. Asquith (never a teetotaller himself, although also probably never deserving his sobriquet 'Squiff').

Backing on to the **Belgian War Memorial** is *Lutyens'* 1930 memorial to **Major-General Lord Cheylesmore [21]**, Victorian soldier, doer of many public good works and a principal promoter of the excellence of Bisley as a rifle shooting centre. *Thomas Brock's* 1880 bronze of **Robert Raikes [22]**, the eighteenth-century founder of Sunday schools, stands to one side in front of the Savoy Hotel. Between **Cheylesmore** and **Raikes** is a bronze relief bust by *Mary Grant*, in 1896, commemorating **Henry Fawcett [23]**, 'Erected to [his] memory by his grateful countrywomen'. **Fawcett** was a Victorian radical politician and laissez-faire economist, blinded early in life in a shooting accident; among the many causes that he espoused was female emancipation.

If you look up from the gardens and away from the river, roughly between **Burns** and **Lawson**, you will see the pretty hideous 1930s office block, the **New Adelphi [24]**, which replaced the *Adam* brothers' eighteenth-century Palladian masterpiece, the residential Adelphi Terrace ('adelphi' meaning brothers in Greek). The two wings projecting towards the gardens have four giant relief figures at their corners, at first-floor level above the terrace, the sculptors (from west to east) being *D. Gilbert, Gilbert Ledward, A. J. J. Ayres* and *Edward Bainbridge Copnall*.

Towards the east end of the gardens, directly in front of the Savoy Hotel's river entrance stands, appropriately, the **D'Oyly Carte Memorial [25]** of 1989, erected to commemorate the centenary of the founding of the hotel by Richard D'Oyly Carte, who eight years earlier had also begun the adjoining Savoy Theatre, with which the names Gilbert and Sullivan are so inextricably associated. Only a few yards off (behind you on your left, as you face the Savoy) stands the **Arthur Sullivan Memorial [26]**. The 1903 bronze bust of Sullivan (who died in 1900) by *William Goscombe John* is itself immemorable, but the sculptor's apparent afterthought – the grieving muse with abandoned lyre, languorously draped round the pedestal – is rightly said to make this quite the most erotic monument in London.

As you leave this section of the gardens at the Waterloo Bridge end, there stands in front of the Institute of Electrical Engineers a 1988 bronze copy of the Royal Institution's original marble of **Michael Faraday [27]**, the inventor of electricity, begun by *John Foley* and (like the **Albert Memorial**, see page 22) finished after *Foley's* death by *Thomas Brock*.

Immediately upstream of Waterloo Bridge, on the Embankment wall, is a bronze relief commemorating **Sir Walter Besant [28]**, who died in 1901. He was a novelist, philanthropist, historian and founder of the Society of Authors. The sculptor of this monument, 'erected by his grateful brethren in literature', was *George Frampton* in 1902.

Beyond Waterloo Bridge

Walk under Waterloo Bridge and you will pass by Somerset House; note a fine pair of lions couchant above the riverside vehicle entrance.

Continue along the Embankment, and at the Temple Place junction you will find *Carlo Marochetti's* bronze of **Isambard Kingdom Brunel [29]** (see illustration, below). Brunel and his contemporary Robert Stephenson (born within three years of each other, both men died within a single month in 1859) are the best-known of the early Victorian civil, and in particular railway, engineers. To Brunel we owe the Great Western Railway, Clifton and Saltash bridges and Paddington and Bristol Temple Meads stations; but also, in a completely different sphere of engineering and design, the *Great Western*, *Great Britain* (restored and now located, appropriately, in Bristol) and *Great Eastern* steamships. This statue was commissioned in the 1860s, as part of a pair with Stephenson (whose statue by *Marochetti* is at Euston Station, see page 117). It was originally intended for the sites in Parliament Square now occupied by **Smuts** and **Palmerston** (see page 50). However, the Office of Works, which had previously exiled **Jenner** from Trafalgar Square (see page 20), had a change of heart and decreed that Parliament Square was to be reserved for statesmen. **Brunel**, therefore, spent some years in the crypt of the Whitehall Chapel and was only erected on this spot in 1877. It is a statue that depicts a man of distinction and dignity, but it lacks the hands-on energy that is so apparent from the best-known photographs of Brunel in his stove-pipe hat. (He is also commemorated by *John Doubleday's* more recent statue next to Platform 1 at Paddington Station, although that falls outside the scope of the walks in this book.)

Towards the City of London

Continue westwards, and just beyond Temple Station, in the final section of Embankment Gardens, you will meet an oddly assorted trio: *Henry Pinker's* 1890 bronze of **W. E. Forster [30]** – Quaker, Member of Parliament, educational reformer and chief promoter of the 1870 Elementary Education Act, which made provision for universal compulsory state education; *Thomas Woolner's* 1878 bronze of a seated **John Stuart Mill [31]**, the eminent Victorian philosopher, as intellectually precocious in his youth as William Pitt the Younger, who died in the year of Mills' birth; and the small bronze of a young girl which, as a bird bath and drinking fountain, is a monument to **Lady (Isabella) Henry Somerset [32]** (1851–1921) and 'temperance'. Lady Henry was one of those redoubtable Victorian crusaders – her own crusade being temperance. In the words of the ODNB 'Her beauty, her eloquence, her power to hold and move great audiences, won for her a widespread reputation', notably as President of the British Women's Temperance Association from 1890 to 1903. During that time, she also founded Duxhurst, near Reigate, as a farm colony for inebriate women. Her monument too, perhaps not inappropriately, became 'legless'. *G. E. Wade's* original 1897 bronze was stolen in 1971, when it was sawn off at the feet, and was only replaced with the present copy some twenty years later. The low plinth bears the delightfully inappropriate inscription 'I was thirsty and ye gave me drink'.

Cross the road to the riverside and on the Embankment wall, opposite the downstream end of the last section of the gardens, another bronze relief bust by *George Frampton* (in 1913) commemorates **William Thomas Stead [33]**, who died in 1912. The inscription records that 'This memorial to a journalist of wide renown was erected near the spot where he worked for more than 30 years by journalists of many lands in recognition of his brilliant gifts, fervent spirit and untiring devotion to the service of his fellow men'. The relief is supported by two delightful little figurines – a knight in armour representing fortitude and a robed maiden as sympathy.

From City to City

As you continue eastwards and downstream you pass out of the City of Westminster and into the City of London – 'the City' proper. As on other main roads into the City, the boundary is marked by two griffins of 1849, brought here in 1963 from the Victorian City Coal Exchange in Lower Thames Street.

The Exchange was demolished that year, ostensibly for road-widening, although in fact its site was not redeveloped for another fifteen years. John Betjeman was an ardent campaigner in the lost cause for the preservation of both the Coal Exchange and the Doric Arch at Euston, which fell – greatly lamented – to the ball and chain of vandalistic modernity at much the same time, although you will meet a double tribute to a successful Betjeman preservation campaign on page 119.

A bronze portrait plaque of **Queen Victoria [34]** by *Charles Mabey* in 1902, immediately behind the 'inshore' griffin, records The Queen's last visit to the City, on 7 March 1900. On the Embankment wall, the **National Submarine War Memorial [35]** of 1922, designed by *A. H. Ryan Tenison* and with relief figures by *F. Brook Hitch*, is a moving tribute to the Royal Navy's Submarine Service, which lost fifty boats during the Great War and another eighty-two during the Second World War.

Blackfriars Bridge

This walk concludes at the north end of Blackfriars Bridge. On the downstream side, just outside the exit from the Underground station, is the **Drinking Fountain [36]**, with a figure of 'Temperance' or possibly another **Woman of Samaria**. It was originally erected outside the Royal Exchange in July 1861 by The Metropolitan Free Drinking Fountains Association. The classically draped, almost decent, rather solemn maiden, sculpted by *Messrs Wills Bros.*, is pouring water from an amphora, or rather not pouring water, since yet another London fountain's active life seems to have expired. The fountain was displaced from the Royal Exchange in 1911 by a new fountain marking the association's Golden Jubilee (the association having in the meantime, in 1867, added Cattle Troughs to its name and remit), see page 96.

To the north-west of the bridge approach is Unilever House, completed in 1932, described by Pevsner as the largest of the City's interwar prestige headquarter buildings. It is still the head office of the Unilever empire, after substantial refurbishment around 1980 and then complete gutting and rebuilding within the listed exterior since the millennium. It is adorned with several interesting sculptural works, all dating from the original building, the additions from the 1980 refurbishment having been removed in the course of the most recent rebuilding. The most conspicuous, carved in Portland stone, are over the entrances at either end of the quadrant river facade: two huge plough horses, each being restrained by lightly clad figures – by two women at the river end and two men at the north end. These are *William Reid Dick's* **Controlled Energy [37]**.

Also from the original building are the **Merman and Mermaid Keystones [38]** by *Gilbert Ledward* over the same entrance doors – the Merman at the north end and the Mermaid at the river end – and the two bronze **Lamp Standards [39]** by *Walter Gilbert*, with their relief panels. From the 1980s refurbishment *Bernard Sindall's* **Abundance** over the former main entrance on the north side has been lost. It was a gilt resin cast of a garlanded girl in a dress, symbolizing fruitfulness and abundance, an allusion to Unilever as a universal provider. The parapet above the quadrant has lost the eight fibreglass resin statues by *Nicholas Monro* of **Japanese**, **Nigerian and English Girls**, representing the 'three ethnic groups of the world' and again symbolizing Unilever's global reach.

In the middle of the footings of the bridge stands a statue of **Queen Victoria [40]**, an 1896 posthumous (of the sculptor) cast of the bronze by *Charles Birch* and erected here by the Corporation of London (the City's governing body) to mark the Diamond Jubilee of 1897. It is an unflattering, but very imperial, image of the Queen Empress.

And finally, as it is such a conspicuous oddity in these bland surroundings, you can hardly miss **The Blackfriar [41]**, on the north-east approach to the bridge, at the bottom of Queen Victoria Street. A rather small and humdrum City public house of 1873, on the site of the former Dominican Priory which disappeared in 1539 on the dissolution of the monasteries under Henry VIII, The Blackfriar was given a complete 'arts and crafts' or art nouveau makeover in 1903–5. The exterior bronzework and the corner statue of a rather jolly (black) friar were the work of *Henry Poole* and the interior makes for a very convenient end to this walk.

To reach Mansion House Underground Station, turn right into Queen Victoria Street. Continue walking and just as you reach the junction with Cannon Street you will come to the Underground station.

8. CITY APPROACHES – FROM SOMERSET HOUSE TO ST PAUL'S

START   Temple Underground Station (Circle and District lines)

FINISH   St Paul's Underground Station (Central line)

DISTANCE   3 km (1 3/4 miles)

DURATION   1 hour

Even though most of London's Underground railway system is barely a hundred years old, it has a good smattering of redundant and closed stations. On the central section of the Piccadilly line, for example, between South Kensington and Green Park, Brompton Road and Down Street stations were closed many years ago, although their distinctive Piccadilly line architecture above ground saves them from complete oblivion. A little further east on the same line, Aldwych is a more recent addition to the list of closures. A tiny station on the south side of the Aldwych crescent, it was latterly served only by a part-time branch line service from Holborn, but it was conveniently adjacent to the starting point of this walk, at Somerset House. However, it too is no longer in service, save as an occasional film set.

Somerset House

But all is not lost. You will begin this walk instead at Temple Underground station, on the Embankment. Turn right out of the station onto the Embankment and head west towards Waterloo Bridge. At the Temple Place junction you will pass a bronze of **Isambard Kingdom Brunel** (see page 79). Just a little further along on your right, enter Somerset House by the river entrance. The first palace of that name was begun in the middle of the sixteenth century by Edward Seymour, the 1st Duke of Somerset, but the buildings that you see today are largely the late eighteenth-century work of *William Chambers*, built principally as government offices and in particular to house the Navy Office. Until the 1830s the Strand Block on the north side also housed the Royal Academy and the Royal Society, until they departed to Burlington House. The 1860s saw the departure of the Navy Office, and until near the end of the twentieth century the principal occupants of the entire complex were the Inland Revenue and the records of the Family Division (as it now is) of the High Court: if you wanted to find a birth certificate or to inspect a will, you went to Somerset House.

Fortunately, at the end of the twentieth century, the ebb of the cultural tide at Somerset House was reversed. The Family Division's records have all moved out, the Inland Revenue has been confined to little more than *James Pennethorne's* separate block on the west side of *Chambers'* palace and the civil servants' car park that blighted the central courtyard has been displaced. The Courtauld Institute's art collection has reoccupied the former premises of the Royal Academy in the Strand Block.

Amid all this architectural splendour you have come to see just one statue, but it is a statue that is the commanding focal point of the vast and elegant central courtyard of the palace. This is the

1789 bronze by *John Bacon Sr* of **George III [1]** (see illustration, below). In contrast to *Matthew Cotes Wyatt's* later mounted statue of **George III** on the west side of Trafalgar Square (see page 62), this is a younger, more flamboyant, more classical king, above a recumbent Father Thames, who is also in bronze and appears to be laden with a cornucopia of fruit salad. In the late nineteenth century the lower part of the pedestal beneath the King was turned into a public urinal that survived some forty years, until it was removed at the outraged instigation of *Aston Webb* (the architect of the **Victoria Memorial**, see page 36).

Around the Aldwych

Leave Somerset House by the Strand gateway on the north side of the courtyard, and you will find yourself back in the bustle of the Aldwych. Cross over the Strand and walk up into India Place (formerly the north end of Montreal Place). On the west side of India House, the seat of the Indian High Commission, is a 1990 bronze bust of **Jawaharlal Nehru [2]** by *Lati Kalcatt*. Nehru was the first Prime Minister of independent India and was followed in that office by two successive generations of his remarkable family – his daughter Indira Gandhi and her son Rajiv Gandhi.

Retrace your steps back to the Strand then turn left and walk eastwards. At the east end of the Aldwych crescent you find *Hamo Thornycroft's* 1905 bronze of the 'Grand Old Man', **William Gladstone [3]**. A Member of Parliament for over sixty years, and Prime Minister on four separate occasions between 1868 and his final resignation in 1894, Gladstone was the colossus of British politics in the Victorian era. He first entered Parliament as a Tory in 1832 and left it as one of the most celebrated – probably *the* most celebrated – of all Liberal statesmen. Although it is in his later uncompromisingly Liberal phase that he is best remembered, this statue portrays him on the political cusp, as it were, in the official robes of a nineteenth-century Chancellor of the Exchequer, to which office he was first appointed in 1852 as a member of the Peelite Tory minority in Lord Aberdeen's Peelite-Whig coalition. Around the base are four subordinate bronzes, representing brotherhood, education, aspiration and courage. The whole work was unveiled by John Morley, another distinguished Victorian Liberal politician, who was the official biographer of Gladstone and one of the two ministers who resigned from Asquith's cabinet on the declaration of war in 1914.

Behind Gladstone is St Clement Danes, the central church of the RAF and the principal commemorative centre of the Royal Air Force, apart from the memorials that can be found on the Embankment (see page 75). The church is itself full of RAF memorials. Other commemorative RAF plaques are set in the paving stones immediately outside the south side of the church. Between the west door and **Gladstone** are statues of two standing figures, both by *Faith Winter*. To the south is her 1988 statue of **Air Chief Marshal Lord Dowding [4]**, commander-in-chief of Fighter Command in 1940, architect of the RAF's victory against the Luftwaffe in the Battle of Britain and arguably the man most responsible for Britain not having lost the war outright in that year.

To the north is a 1992 figure of **Marshal of the Royal Air Force Sir Arthur Harris [5]**, Commander-in-Chief of Bomber Command for most of the war and the principal architect of the still contentious strategy of seeking to bomb Germany into submission. Their admirers have claimed that both men were less than well treated by an ungrateful nation. Dowding was summarily sacked after the Battle of Britain and was denied promotion to a Marshalship of the RAF. Harris did not receive the peerage awarded to many of his colleagues in wartime military high office, and has been vilified as a war criminal for his bombing policy. It may therefore have been some small posthumous consolation that both statues were unveiled by HM Queen Elizabeth, the Queen Mother.

Stand among the three statues and, like them, look back to the west. You are facing the east end and main entrance of Australia House, the early twentieth-century centre of Australian representation in London. Two huge groups of stone figures by *Harold Parker*, himself an Australian, flank the doorway. Of the same period (1915), but only installed well after the Great War (in 1924), is the bronze group high up above the cornice, representing **Phoebus and the Horses of the Sun [6]**. This is by *Bertram Mackennal*, also an Australian, whose **Edward VII** can be seen on the walk on pages 34–45.

Outside the east end of St Clement Danes is a quite different work: a life-sized statue of **Doctor Johnson [7]** (see illustration, right), the gift of its sculptor, *Percy Fitzgerald*, in 1910. St Clement Danes was Dr Johnson's parish church, and you will be meeting him again very shortly. Johnson – fulsomely if also entirely justifiably described as 'critic, essayist, philologist, biographer, wit, poet, moralist, dramatist, political writer, talker' – is also commemorated by *John Bacon Sr's* statue inside St Paul's, although that falls outside the scope of these walks. His was the first statue to be erected in St Paul's, a tribute organized by his friend and contemporary Sir Joshua Reynolds.

Fleet Street

Continue eastwards along the Strand, past the Royal Courts of Justice. The Strand becomes Fleet Street at *Horace Jones's* **Temple Bar Memorial [8]**, marking the western boundary of the City of London and the site of the former Temple Bar. Like Hyde Park Corner, Temple Bar – a stone archway across the street – had become a notorious Victorian traffic bottleneck. It was removed in 1878–9 and replaced the following year by the present memorial. The two principal statues, of Queen Victoria and the Prince of Wales (later Edward VII), are by *Edgar Boehm*, the traditional City griffin by *Charles Birch* and the north- and south-side reliefs commemorating the Queen's visits to the City by, respectively, *Charles Kelsey* and *Charles Mabey*. *Jones* himself was the City architect and surveyor at the time and was also responsible for the City's three principal food markets – Smithfield, Leadenhall and Billingsgate – and for the former City Lunatic Asylum at

Dartford. You will see the old Temple Bar itself later in the walk in Paternoster Square on the north side of St Paul's (see page 88).

Continue eastwards and beyond Chancery Lane on the north side of Fleet Street is St Dunstan-in-the-West, an early nineteenth-century rebuilding whose unassuming facade conceals an unusual Gothic octagonal interior. But your interest lies outside, on the street frontage of the church. The clock, which was made by *Thomas Harris* in 1671, was restored to the church in the 1930s. The statue of the first **Queen Elizabeth [9]**, by *William Kerwin*, is believed to have been made in 1586 and was brought here in 1760 from its original site at Ludgate, when the latter was demolished to permit road widening. The decayed statues of **King Lud and His Sons [10]**, now in the vestry porch, are also from Ludgate. The two hammer-wielding bellringers are reminiscent of the two moors performing a similar function on the clock tower on the north side of the Piazza San Marco in Venice. **Lord Northcliffe's Memorial [11]**, of 1930, is a bust by *Kathleen Scott* on an obelisk by *Edwin Lutyens*. The

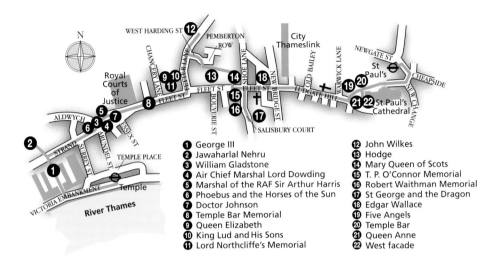

WEST HARDING ST

PEMBERTON ROW

City Thameslink

NEWGATE ST

St Paul's

CHEAPSIDE

Royal Courts of Justice

FLEET ST

LUDGATE HILL

St Paul's Cathedral

ALDWYCH

SALISBURY COURT

TEMPLE PLACE

Temple

VICTORIA EMBANKMENT

River Thames

1 George III
2 Jawaharlal Nehru
3 William Gladstone
4 Air Chief Marshal Lord Dowding
5 Marshal of the RAF Sir Arthur Harris
6 Phoebus and the Horses of the Sun
7 Doctor Johnson
8 Temple Bar Memorial
9 Queen Elizabeth
10 King Lud and His Sons
11 Lord Northcliffe's Memorial

12 John Wilkes
13 Hodge
14 Mary Queen of Scots
15 T. P. O'Connor Memorial
16 Robert Waithman Memorial
17 St George and the Dragon
18 Edgar Wallace
19 Five Angels
20 Temple Bar
21 Queen Anne
22 West facade

remarkable Harmsworth brothers, respectively the first Lords Northcliffe and Rothermere, were two of the great press 'barons', in every sense, of the early twentieth century.

A Champion and a Cat

Just past the church turn left and walk up Fetter Lane on the left-hand side. This takes you to an earlier champion of the press, **John Wilkes [12]**, whose standing bronze at the junction of Fetter Lane and New Fetter Lane is by *James Butler* in 1988. Wilkes is most widely remembered today as a 'champion of free speech' and his issues of *The New Briton* and the battles royal between the electors of Middlesex and the House of Commons over Wilkes's entitlement to take up his parliamentary seat in the early 1760s were a watershed in the development of English press freedoms. Although he was one of the most outspoken men of his time, he was not a demagogue; a libertine and member of Sir Francis Dashwood's notorious Hellfire Club, it is true, yet also a man of wit and erudition; the darling of the London mob in the 1760s, but also a distinguished Lord Mayor in 1774 and a staunch defender of the Establishment in the Gordon Riots of 1780. Now that all the national newspapers have moved elsewhere, Wilkes's statue is one of the few remaining indications of Fleet Street's historic connection with the press.

Return down Fetter Lane on the east side, and make your way to Gough Square by turning left into West Harding Street, and at its other end turning right into Gough Square. In the square you will find Doctor Johnson's House on your right and opposite it, on a low waist-high plinth, **Hodge [13]**, Dr Johnson's cat, a 1997 bronze by *Jon Bickley*. Hodge, in his owner's words recorded on the plinth, was 'A very fine cat indeed', and the work is made all the more charming by the nice conceit of Hodge being seated on Dr Johnson's dictionary in company with two oysters, which his owner was wont to feed him (the sculptor used Norfolk oysters to add authenticity to his depiction of Hodge's feast).

Besides Dr Johnson's famous encomium of London – 'Sir, when a man is tired of London he is tired of life: for there is in London all that life can afford' – the plinth also records the statue's commemoration of Major Byron F. Caws, who assisted H. W. Fowler in the preparation of the first edition of the *Concise Oxford Dictionary*, and by whose grandson Richard the statue was gifted to the Corporation of London. Nowadays **Hodge** the statue has become as much of a local character as his feline forebear, with Christmas tinsel and a kilt on Burns Night, among other good-natured attention.

Fleet Street Revisited

Now return to Fleet Street for three little curiosities. Leave the square at the east end, and follow Hind Court down to Fleet Street. On the north side, shortly before the imposing facades of the former *Daily Telegraph* and *Daily Express* buildings, is an Edwardian office building called Queen of Scots House. The statue by an unknown hand of **Mary Queen of Scots [14]**, seen in a niche at first-floor level, rather incongruously lodged over a Pret A Manger and next to Ye Olde Cheshire Cheese, was instigated by the developer, Sir John Tollemache Sinclair MP – somewhat romantically, since Mary is thought never even to have visited London, let alone Fleet Street.

On the south side of Fleet Street, more or less opposite the former *Daily Telegraph* building on a small stone support, is the **T. P. O'Connor Memorial [15]**, a 1935 bronze by *F. W. Doyle-Jones* (who was also responsible for the statuary at the entrance to Waterloo Station) on the front of the old *News Chronicle* building. It commemorates the journalist, parliamentary correspondent, Member of Parliament, Father of the House (the longest serving member in the House of Commons) and first President of the Board of Film Censors – a richly varied assortment.

A few steps east along Fleet Street, turn right into Salisbury Court, and proceed to Salisbury Square and the **Robert Waithman Memorial [16]**. It is a Devon-granite obelisk honouring the early nineteenth-century radical common councillor and City Member of Parliament, and Lord Mayor of 1823–4, erected in the year of his death in 1833.

Continuing south from the square, in Dorset Rise, is a modern sculptural work. This is *Michael Sandle's* 1988 bronze of **St George and the Dragon [17]**, which is a far cry from *Adrian Jones's* version of the same subject matter in the Cavalry Memorial in Hyde Park (see page 17). It is an almost painfully harsh and brutal representation.

St Paul's

Return to Ludgate Circus, from where the partial view of the west end of St Paul's has been greatly improved since the removal of the old railway viaduct and the relocation of the Thameslink railway line underground (the resulting downhill run from Blackfriars Station to St Paul's Thameslink Station is the steepest incline anywhere on the British railway network). At Ludgate Circus, on the north-west corner, is a 1934 bronze tablet with a relief portrait commemorating **Edgar Wallace [18]**, journalist and best-selling author, and probably the first newspaper vendor (one of his early trades) to receive a national monument. Walk up Ludgate Hill (on the south side, in anticipation of a slightly better view) to the west side of St Paul's Churchyard. You are facing the recently and pristinely cleaned west front of *Sir Christopher Wren's* greatest masterpiece, St Paul's Cathedral.

Immediately to your left as you stand on the zebra crossing, facing the cathedral, is Juxon House, at the south-west corner of the recently redeveloped Paternoster Square complex. (If you are interested in passing through Paternoster Square see the walk on pages 100–9). On free-standing columns forming part of the Juxon House arcade are five stone heads – **Five Angels [19]** – by *Emily Young*. The work is in her very distinctively characteristic style: huge, powerful, visually striking, almost primeval, but also a most appropriate and pleasing complement to the new Juxon House, and unveiled in December 2003 after completion of the redevelopment. *Emily Young's* grandmother was *Kathleen Scott*, who was herself a pupil of *Rodin*, which is a nice artistic link.

Between Juxon House and the new Cathedral Shop on the west side of *Wren's* Chapter House (which itself has somehow managed to survive all the demolition and development vicissitudes of the rest of Paternoster Square) is the original **Temple Bar [20]**. Replacing its wooden predecessor, which was badly damaged in the Great Fire of 1666, **Temple Bar** was commissioned by Charles II, designed (it is said, even if uncertainly) by *Wren* and erected between 1669 and 1672 on the spot at the west end of Fleet Street now commemorated by the **Temple Bar Memorial** that you saw earlier on this walk. By 1800 all the other principal gateways into the City – Aldgate, Aldersgate, Bishopsgate, Cripplegate, Ludgate, Moorgate and Newgate – had been demolished. **Temple Bar** survived until 1878, when the demands of Victorian traffic necessitated its removal.

Fortunately, rather than being demolished, it was dismantled and its stones stored. In 1880, the brewer Sir Henry Meux bought the ensemble and re-erected the arch as a gateway at his estate, Theobalds Park, in Hertfordshire, where it remained for the next 120 years. In 1984 it was bought by the Temple Bar Trust from the Meux Trust for £1. In 2003 it was carefully dismantled for a second time and re-erected on the south side of Paternoster Square, its original east-west orientation being turned to a north-south axis. The restored Bar, incorporating over 95 per cent of the original stonework, was ceremonially reopened – quite literally, by the pushing open of the two wooden gates, which weigh over a ton apiece – by the Lord Mayor on 10 November 2004. In brilliantly cleaned Portland stone, with *John Bushnell's* original statues of **Charles I** and **Charles II** above the south side of the archway and **James I** and his queen, **Anne of Denmark**, on the north side, and with *Tim Crawley's* new **Lion and Unicorn** on the south side and **City Griffins** on the north, all holding their new heraldic cartouches, it is a stunningly successful adornment of the new redevelopment, besides being a wonderful rescue and restoration of one of the most famous City monuments.

Before the west front of the cathedral, on her own central island site, stands **Queen Anne [21]** (see illustration, right) (not to be confused with her great-grandmother commemorated on **Temple Bar**). This is an 1886 marble copy by *Richard Belt* and (principally) *Louis Malempré* of the 1712 original by *Francis Bird*, which was part of *Wren's* design for the west front and its surrounds, but which was badly vandalized during the later part of the eighteenth century and eventually replaced by the Corporation of London with the 1886 copy. *Bird's* original, also in marble, is now at St Mary's Place, Holmhurst in Sussex. Surrounding the plinth are four subordinate statues, all female, representing Britain, North America, France and Ireland. Apart from being a tactful tribute to the reigning monarch, the whole group was also something of an expression of nationalistic triumphalism in celebration of the completion of

the rebuilding of the City's then largest edifice (the first stone of the new cathedral having been laid in 1675, with the whole building being declared complete by Parliament in 1711), the successes of Marlborough's wars and the stability of the then still infant United Kingdom – the Act of Union of the Kingdoms of England and Scotland and their respective Parliaments having been passed only as recently as 1707.

The overall ensemble of the sculpture on the exterior of the cathedral itself is described by Pevsner as 'The greatest such ensemble of the English Baroque', and indeed, as you stand in front of **Queen Anne**, much of the other statuary that you can see on the **west facade [22]** is also by *Francis Bird*: the **Conversion of St Paul** in the west pediment, of 1706; the seven reliefs of scenes from the **Life of St Paul** round the west door, mostly of 1711–14; and the statues of the four seated evangelists at the bases of the two towers, of 1720–3.

Proceed round the north side of the cathedral to the north-east corner of the precinct. On your left, at the junction of Newgate Street, Cheapside and St Martin's le Grand, there are entrances to St Paul's Underground Station.

9. OLD CITY – FROM ST PAUL'S TO THE MONUMENT

START	St Paul's Underground Station (Central line)
FINISH	Monument Underground Station (Circle and District lines; linked to Bank Underground Station, Central and Northern lines)
DISTANCE	3.7 km (2 ¼ miles)
DURATION	1 ¼ hours

This walk begins outside the north transept of St Paul's Cathedral, which is barely a stone's throw from St Paul's Underground Station. Even in that short distance, however, the infrequent visitor to the City may wonder at the changes in recent years to the City's townscape: the unloved 1960s *Holford* development in Paternoster Square has gone completely; the 1980s British Telecom Centre sits on the site of the former 1870s West Range of the General Post Office, flanked by King Edward Street, Newgate Street and St Martin's le Grand; and more than half the buildings in that last street have been completely redeveloped in the last decade. The block surrounded by New Change, Cheapside, Bread Street and Watling Street is now a colossal building site. St Paul's itself, however, stands unchanged after three hundred years – an age that seems all the more astonishing when compared with the remarkably short lifespans of many of the cathedral's commercial neighbours, and even more so when one considers its remarkable survival of the German Blitz, which is commemorated by a statue that you will see early on in this walk. You will see a similar mix of old and new as you walk through the heart of the City, ending at the Monument, the memorial to the even older city that was so devastated by the Great Fire of 1666.

St Paul's Cathedral

Outside the north transept stands a 1988 lifesize bronze of **John Wesley [1]**, the founder of the Methodist Societies, cast from the original 1849 marble by *Samuel Manning, Father and Son*, which now stands in Westminster Central Hall, the 'headquarters' of Methodism. The statue is, very obviously and appropriately, of a preacher. A few feet away to the east, as a large raised plaque set into the paving, is *Richard Kindersley's* 1999 Irish limestone **Memorial to the Londoners Killed in Bombardments During World War II [2]**, commemorating in particular the thirty thousand Londoners killed in air raids during the war.

Continuing clockwise around the cathedral, you come to both the stone commemorating the old St Paul's Cross – a wooden cross where sermons were preached and that was removed after several hundred years in 1643 – and the present **St Paul's Cross [3]** (of 1910), a bronze by *Bertram Mackennal* on a Portland-stone column and black marble base designed by *Reginald Blomfield*. The railings along this north side of the precinct date back to 1714 and are an early example of English cast iron.

91

Further still round the cathedral, just tucked into the south-east angle of the quire and the south transept, is *Edward Bainbridge Copnall's* 1971 statue of **Becket [4]**. He was Chancellor of England, Archbishop of Canterbury and saint; a unique combination in English history, making Becket the most famous of all the 104 Archbishops of Canterbury. It is a resin bronze, erected in 1973 but commemorating the eight hundredth anniversary of Becket's murder in Canterbury Cathedral in 1170. Most unusually for a commemorative figurative statue, but also most effectively, Becket is represented on the ground, at the point of death. Becket's connection with the City is that he was born in a house in Cheapside, probably on the site of the present Mercers' Hall. In fact, the offices above Mercers' Hall are called Becket House and there is a small modern bronze relief of Becket on the south-west corner of the building.

Around Cannon Street

Leave the cathedral precinct on its south side and cross the road to the top of the pedestrian walkway leading from the south transept straight down to the Millenium Bridge, with Tate Modern in the old Bankside Power Station on the south side of the bridge. At the top of the walkway is **Blitz [5]** (see illustration, right), *John W. Mills's* bronze in honour of all the London firefighters killed in the Blitz (the German bombing of London during World War II, and in particular during the winter of 1940/1). Originally unveiled by the Queen Mother in 1991 as the London firefighters' memorial, it was rededicated and unveiled by the Princess Royal in 2003 as the United Kingdom Firefighters National Memorial. Three firemen, in tin helmets and with their high-pressure hose, provide a convincing representation of the activity and drama of wartime firefighting.

Proceed a short way east from **Blitz** to Old Change Court, the grassed open area to your right. At the far end, overlooking *Wren's* St Nicholas Cole Abbey, is *Michael Ayrton's* 1973 bronze of **Icarus [6]**, flexing his wings before take-off. (If you complete the walk on pages 73–81, compare this with the Daedalus element of *James Butler's* **Fleet Air Arm Memorial**).

Continue east to Cannon Street, and to Bracken House, built in the late 1950s for the *Financial Times* by *Albert Richardson*, and rebuilt around 1990 by *Michael Hopkins* between the preserved original north and south blocks. The original building has the distinction of being the first post-war building to be listed (in 1987) or accorded special protection under the Planning Acts. Our interest, however, is confined to one tiny feature: the extravagantly ornate **Zodiacal Clock [7]** above the main north entrance, by *Frank Dobson* and *Philip Bentham*, and in particular the features of Churchill (in whose wartime government the then chairman of the *Financial Times*, Brendan Bracken, had served as a minister) in lieu of Apollo in the central bronze sun.

Cross Cannon Street, and return a little to the west to the Festival Gardens immediately outside the south-east entrance into the cathedral precinct. The gardens, also by *Albert Richardson*, were part of the City's contribution to the Festival of Britain in 1951, whose most enduring legacy is the Festival Hall on the South Bank. The wall fountain was the gift of the Gardeners' Company, one of the livery companies of the City, now 107 in number and ranging from the medieval Mercers to the rather more contemporary Tax Advisers and Taxi Drivers. Immediately behind the fountain is *Georg Ehrlich's* **The Young Lovers [8]**, a 1951 bronze but only erected here in 1969, portraying a slim, seated couple, embracing sideways.

On the other side of New Change (which adjoins the east end of Festival Gardens), at the corner of Watling Street, is the **Memorial to Admiral Arthur Phillip [9]**, who led the First Fleet and founded the penal settlement in Sydney Harbour that was the genesis of modern Australia. Sydney takes its name from Thomas Townshend, 1st Viscount Sydney, Secretary of State for the Home Department, whose jurisdiction at that time included the colonies. The date of Phillips's landing at Port Jackson, Saturday 26 January 1788, is commemorated every year as Australia Day. The original 1932 bust by *C. L. Hartwell* was first installed in St Mildred's Bread Street, but after wartime damage, found its way to St Mary-le-Bow in Cheapside.

Continue east along Watling Street, which is unrelated to the Roman road running north-west across Middle England, but is a modern corruption of the Old English *Aethelingstrate*. Just past Bow Lane, now a pedestrianized shopping street, is *Alma Boyes'* **The Cordwainer [10]** of 2002, a seated bronze of a shoemaker, with a finely worked face and head. The name has nothing to do with cord, or even corduroy, but is derived from Cordoba in Spain, reputedly the source of the finest medieval leather. The word itself – pretty much synonymous with 'shoemaker' – is now archaic, but still survives thanks to the livery company of that name.

The Cordwainer Connection

Cross over the road, walk west along Watling Street a short way and then turn right into Bow Lane. A left turn by Bow Wine Vaults brings you into Bow Churchyard, which like the previous statue, falls within the Ward of Cordwainer. You will find here *Charles Rennick's* 1960 replica in bronze of *William Couper's* original 1907 bronze in Richmond, Virginia, of **Captain John Smith [11]**, himself a member of the Cordwainers' Company. As the inscription on the pediment records, Smith was 'First among the leaders of the settlement at Jamestown, Virginia from which began the overseas expansion of the English speaking peoples', more than four hundred years ago. Smith, a generation younger than the better-known Elizabethan buccaneers and explorers, had a colourful 'Flashmanesque' pedigree in his youth, but he also made a serious and substantial contribution to the survival and success of the Virginian settlement. He also advised, but did not accompany, the later expedition of the Pilgrim Fathers to Massachusetts. A material factor in the choice of Bow Churchyard for the statue was the Cordwainer connection.

Cross over Bow Lane, walk to the top and then turn right into Cheapside. At the east end of Cheapside, which runs into Poultry, immediately

before Mansion House – the official residence of the Lord Mayor – turn right into Walbrook. Walk to the junction with Cannon Street where, uniquely, at least within the scope of this book, the mobile telephone is commemorated in bronze. **The LIFFE Trader [12]** is a striped-blazered, ID-card-tagged, mobile-telephoned London International Financial Futures Exchange trader by *Stephen Melton* in 1997, the sculptor's own details being recorded – a nice conceit – on the trader's sculpted ID tag.

Walk back up Walbrook. You will pass St Stephen Walbrook church on your right. The controversial altar by *Henry Moore*, commissioned by Lord Palumbo as part of his very generous rescue and restoration in the 1980s of this, one of *Wren's* largest churches, falls outside the scope of this outdoor walk, but you may wish to make a quick visit.

The Bank of England

Walbrook leads you into Poultry, with *George Dance the Elder's* Mansion House on your right at the junction. If you stand in front of the Mansion House, facing away, the **Bank of England [13]** is directly ahead, between Princes Street and Threadneedle Street, with Lothbury and Bartholomew Lane flanking the north and east sides of the bank's island site. The bank's affectionate name, The Old Lady, is thought to date from a Gillray cartoon of 1797 entitled 'Political Ravishment or The Old Lady of Threadneedle Street in Danger'. Indeed, in the central pediment above the main Threadneedle Street frontage sits *Charles Wheeler's* **The Lady of the Bank [14]** (see illustration, right), which replaced the old eighteenth-century Britannia when the bank was reconstructed in the 1920s. The bank was originally the masterpiece of *Soane*, built over a period of nearly forty years from 1788, but its substantial demolition and reconstruction under the direction of *Herbert Baker* a century later were described by Pevsner in 1957 as the greatest act of official vandalism in London during the twentieth century. This is a judgement that his subsequent editors have affirmed forty years later. The most conspicuous external surviving parts of *Soane's* bank are the perimeter walls, although even these were altered by *Baker*, by the removal of many of *Soane's* blind windows and the substitution of the present bronze doors by *Wheeler*.

On the other hand, in the context of these walks, *Baker's* reconstruction has resulted in additional statuary. Below **The Lady of the Bank**, *Wheeler* was also responsible for the six giant figures on the Threadneedle Street frontage, above the lower balustrade: two inner female **caryatids** and four outer male **telamones**, all of 1931: and for **The Lothbury Ladies [15]**, the four stone female figures of 1937 on the Lothbury frontage.

If you proceed clockwise round the perimeter of the bank, Tivoli Corner was one of the most celebrated features of *Soane's* bank, the design being based on the Temple of Vesta at Tivoli. This too was altered by *Baker*, the corner becoming an open rotunda with a new copper roof, topped by a gilded and gleaming **Ariel [16]**, also by *Charles Wheeler*. In one sense, the principal visible surviving monument to *Soane* is *William Reid Dick's* 1937 stone statue of **Sir John Soane [17]** in the west niche on the Lothbury frontage.

Bank

Bank is not just the geographical centre of the City. You are in the middle of the oldest of the world's great financial trading centres, and at the same time at the heart of both the City itself and of London. This is particularly the case now that the business and commerce of London stretch not only westwards to the West End and beyond, but also eastwards to the almost alien grid pattern

and skyscrapers of Canary Wharf. All main roads into London ultimately lead to Bank, even if distances to London's centre are measured to Charing Cross, and also even if it is a little difficult to associate Newgate Street with the A40 and King William Street with the A3.

The **Mansion House** has been the official residence of the Lord Mayor for over 250 years without a break, while the **Bank of England** has been in continuous business on the same site since 1734. Indeed, a recent security review at the bank led to the delightful discovery that none of the bank's ground-level entrances could be opened from outside: it had never been necessary to open them from outside, because in nearly three hundred years the bank's premises had never been left unattended (indeed, even with the security of *Soane's* wall, the Bank's Picquet, or overnight military guard from the Guards Barracks, was only abolished in 1973). Should a terrorist alert necessitate the complete evacuation of the bank, it was realized access could only be regained by means of a ladder and the window of the Governor's office.

On the west corner of the Bank *rond-point* is the former Poultry office of **National Westminster Bank [18]**, an early 1930s building by *Edwin Cooper*. Briefly note its two pairs of rather undistinguished statues in the ground-floor alcoves on the Cheapside and Princes Street frontages, and the rather larger allegorical ensemble of statuary above the corner parapet by *Ernest Gillick*, being 'Britannia seated between the figures of Higher Mathematics and Lower Mathematics, supported by Mercury and Truth with the Owl of Wisdom in one corner'.

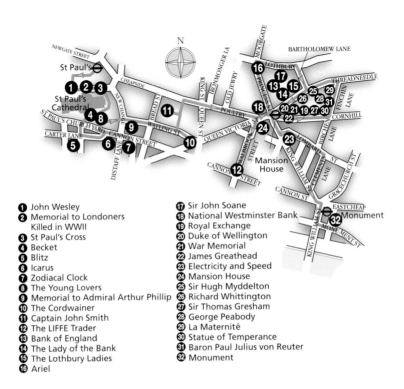

1. John Wesley
2. Memorial to Londoners Killed in WWII
3. St Paul's Cross
4. Becket
5. Blitz
6. Icarus
7. Zodiacal Clock
8. The Young Lovers
9. Memorial to Admiral Arthur Phillip
10. The Cordwainer
11. Captain John Smith
12. The LIFFE Trader
13. Bank of England
14. The Lady of the Bank
15. The Lothbury Ladies
16. Ariel
17. Sir John Soane
18. National Westminster Bank
19. Royal Exchange
20. Duke of Wellington
21. War Memorial
22. James Greathead
23. Electricity and Speed
24. Mansion House
25. Sir Hugh Myddelton
26. Richard Whittington
27. Sir Thomas Gresham
28. George Peabody
29. La Maternité
30. Statue of Temperance
31. Baron Paul Julius von Reuter
32. Monument

Royal Exchange

Besides the **Bank of England** and the **Mansion House**, the third dominant building overlooking this, the heart of the City, is *William Tite's* 1840s **Royal Exchange [19]**, situated between Threadneedle Street and Cornhill. It was built in the 1840s as the second successor to Sir Thomas Gresham's original exchange (the intervening second exchange having been burnt down in 1838). On the triangular open space in front of the **Royal Exchange**, the principal statue, at the apex of the triangle, is *Francis Chantrey's* 1844 mounted bronze of the **Duke of Wellington [20]**, a classical work without stirrups or hat, and a contrast to *Boehm's* later and more conventionally contemporary work opposite Apsley House (see page 31). Although the statue is described as *Chantrey's* work, *Chantrey* died of a heart attack in November 1841 when the statue was still at a relatively early stage of creation, and it was in fact completed by his assistant, *Henry Weekes*. It was unveiled on 18 June 1844, the twenty-ninth anniversary of the Battle of Waterloo.

Behind the Duke and immediately in front of the main facade of the **Royal Exchange** is the **War Memorial [21]** of 1920, designed by *Aston Webb*, with two bronze riflemen sculpted by *Alfred Drury*. It commemorates all officers, non-commissioned officers and soldiers of London who served in both world wars.

On a high plinth in the middle of Cornhill, by the south-west corner of the Exchange, is *James Butler's* 1994 bronze of **James Greathead [22]**. It is a surprisingly recent and, therefore, belated, if also more or less centennial, commemoration of the late Victorian (and South African) chief engineer of the City and South London Railway, whose invention of the cylindrical tunnelling shield significantly helped the construction of a great part of the London Underground railway system. The City and South London was the first of the deep (as opposed to 'cut and cover') underground railway lines, and its first stretch, opened in 1890, ran from Elephant and Castle to King William Street – now part of the eastern section of the Northern Line. The King William Street terminus was unsatisfactory from the outset and the line was soon extended north to Bank and Moorgate.

The ticket office of the first station at Bank was built in the crypt of St Mary Woolnoth, at the junction of Lombard and King William Streets. The single-storey facade of the old station still stands attached to the south side of *Hawksmoor's* church. In the facade's Baroque broken pediment are **Electricity and Speed [23]**, two reclining figures by *Oliver Wheatley* in 1899: **Electricity** is a female figure verging on the hermaphroditic, sparking off a flash of electricity with her pointed finger; **Speed** is represented by Mercury.

Looking back from the **Duke of Wellington** to the **Mansion House [24]**, you can admire the latter's great Corinthian portico and its pediment, carved by *Robert Taylor the Younger*. It shows the personified City of London in the centre trampling 'envy' and receiving from the right side the benefits of 'plenty' brought to London by the River Thames, which is depicted to the left by a recumbent Father Thames. *Taylor* preceded *Soane* as architect to the **Bank of England**, he was also a governor of the Foundling Hospital (see page 115) and instrumental in its design and his considerable fortune funded the Taylorian Institute at Oxford.

From the same spot, in the opposite direction, above the Corinthian portico of the **Royal Exchange**, view the sculpture in the pediment by *Richard Westmacott the Younger,* depicting 'commerce', both personified in the centre and represented in the persons of the flanking individual merchants, with the splendidly Victorian subscription 'The Earth is the Lord's and the fullness thereof'. Along the base of the pediment, the bold gilt inscription *'Anno. Elizabethae. R.XIII. Conditum. Anno. Victoriae. R.VIII. Restauratum'* is a reminder that there has been an exchange on this site for over half a millennium. The steps of the **Royal Exchange** are one of the two sites in the City from which the accession of a new sovereign is proclaimed. This was the younger *Westmacott's* only important public work, but he was sufficiently distinguished to have succeeded his father as professor of sculpture at the Royal Academy.

On the Threadneedle Street frontage of the **Royal Exchange** are two stone statues, both of 1844, in niches at the upper level. To the left, *Samuel Joseph's* **Sir Hugh Myddelton [25]**, Jacobean engineer and projector of the New River, which greatly improved the City's water supply; to the right, *John Carew's* **Richard Whittington [26]**, four times Lord Mayor half a millennium ago and perhaps the best-known Lord Mayor of all, at least to generations of children. In fact, the legend of the orphan Dick Whittington, his cat and the message of Bow bells, 'Turn again Whittington, Lord Mayor of London', only arose two centuries after Whittington's death, and bears little resemblance to the successful politician and mercer of actuality. (You can meet Dick Whittington again at the Guildhall on page 104).

Above the entrance at the far (east) end of the Exchange is *William Behnes'* 1845 stone statue of **Sir Thomas Gresham [27]**, founder of the original Elizabethan exchange. On top of the stone cupola surmounting the campanile is a weathervane in the shape of Gresham's heraldic device, a grasshopper, and the same motif appears as decoration on the cornice round the building.

In the piazza at the far end of the **Exchange**, on a red granite base, the most prominent sculpture is William Wetmore Story's 1869 bronze of **George Peabody [28]**, the American philanthropist and eponymous founder of the charitable housing trust whose extensive estates can still be seen today throughout central London. Story was also an American, living in Rome, where Peabody went for the sculptor's sittings. Just to complete the international pedigree of a statue of one American by another, modelled in Italy and erected in England, the bronze itself was cast in Munich. The statue was unveiled four months before Peabody's death. He died on 4 November 1869.

Just to the north-east of **Peabody** is *Aimé-Jules Dalou's* 1879 **Charity Drinking Fountain** (also known as **La Maternité) [29]** – a delightful mélange of bronze and pink and grey granite. In fact, **Peabody** and the **Fountain** swapped places as recently as the 1980s. On the Cornhill side of the piazza is another drinking fountain (the successor to the displaced Blackfriars **fountain**, see page 81): this one still has the canopy that *Dalou's* fountain has lost, and a sculpture, '**Statue of Temperance**' [30].

Immediately opposite the east entrance to the **Exchange**, below **Sir Thomas Gresham**, is *Michael Black's* 1976 granite head and shoulders of **Baron Paul Julius von Reuter [31]**, commemorating the 125th anniversary of the foundation of the news service that still bears his name and that began its life here in 1851.

Monument

From the south side of Cornhill, go down Birchin Lane, and turn left into Lombard Street, the spiritual home of British banking, where even today the banks' signs hang out across the street (although they only returned with Edward VII's coronation, having been banned by Charles II). There are no outdoor statues to detain you on this street apart from an exotically bare-breasted pair of ladies flanking the sphinx over the extravagantly ornate entrance to Number 24. So think about Walter Bagehot's Victorian description of Lombard Street as 'by far the greatest combination of economical power and economical delicacy that the world has ever seen', or the old saying, 'All Lombard Street to a China orange', implying very long odds, since to stake all the wealth of London against an orange was to stake fabulous riches against a trifle.

As you reach Gracechurch Street, at the east end of Lombard Street, you can see the top of your destination, the **Monument [32]** (see illustration, right), at the junction of Monument Street and Fish Street Hill. On Sunday 2 September 1666, a fire broke out in a baker's house in Pudding Lane, exactly 61 metres (202 feet) to the east. When the fire was finally extinguished three days later, it had destroyed some 13,000 houses, devastated 176 hectares (436 acres) of the City and destroyed or severely damaged numerous churches and public buildings, including the old St Paul's Cathedral. The **Monument**, a colossal Doric column, is the permanent memorial to the Great Fire.

Designed, once again, by *Wren* and his friend and colleague *Robert Hooke*, the column is 61 metres (202 feet) high, topped by a drum and a gilt copper urn spouting flames. Three hundred and eleven steps lead to a viewing platform giving a wonderful panorama not only of the entire City but even as far as the Crystal Palace transmitters and suburban Kent and Surrey – well worth the climb and the puff. At the base of the column, round three sides are Latin inscriptions recording the fire, the restoration of the City and the erection of the **Monument**; on the west side is elaborate allegorical relief sculpture by *Caius Gabriel Cibber* (see pages 21 and 54). After an eighteen-month restoration programme costing £4.5 million, the **Monument** was reopened in February 2009, with its stone exterior cleaned and a new stainless steel safety cage round the viewing platform.

There is an entrance to Monument Underground Station on Fish Street Hill, right by the historic **Monument** itself.

10. NEW CITY – FROM LIVERPOOL STREET TO HOLBORN VIADUCT

START   Liverpool Street Underground Station (Hammersmith & City, Circle, Metropolitan and Central lines; overground services run from Liverpool Street mainline station)

FINISH   Chancery Lane Underground Station (Central line)

DISTANCE   5.4 km (3 1/3 miles)

DURATION   1 1/2 hours

This walk includes a number of more recent sculptural works and passes through some of the more modern parts of the northern half of the City – Broadgate, the Barbican, Paternoster Square and Ludgate. The Barbican is the extraordinary product of the devastation wrought by the wartime Blitz over a vast area north of London Wall. Apart from its Arts Centre, it is a largely residential development, comprising huge amounts of homogenous reinforced concrete. It is functional, soulless and – amazingly – now listed, or protected, under the Planning Acts. Paternoster Square, the area immediately to the north of St Paul's, was also devastated in the Second World War. Here the development cycle has already done an additional round as the present buildings are the second post-war development. Broadgate and Ludgate (the former is a modern name, there was no medieval Broadgate into the City) are both the by-products of the closure of railway stations – Broad Street in

the east and Holborn Viaduct in the west. The 1980s developments on these sites have produced some of the City's bolder office buildings, and through the enlightened patronage of Stuart Lipton and David Blackburn of Rosehaugh Stanhope, the principal developer involved in both projects, Broadgate in particular has been embellished with a considerable amount of modern sculpture.

Outside Liverpool Street Station

This walk begins at Liverpool Street station. Substantially refurbished at the same time as the Broadgate development, its concourse and shops are smart, and on every side it is now bordered by the evident prosperity of the eastern half of the City.

Leave the station at the Liverpool Street exit, now named Hope Square. You immediately meet the 2006 memorial to the **Children of the Kindertransport [1]**, a bronze group of five children and their suitcases, with a short stretch of railway track and plaques bearing the names of German railway stations. The piece, by the sculptor *Frank Meisler* and dedicated by the Association of Jewish Refugees, is expressed to be 'In gratitude to the people of Britain for saving the lives of 10,000 unaccompanied mainly Jewish children who fled from Nazi persecution in 1938 and 1939.'

The next stop is the **Great Eastern Railway Great War Memorial [2]**, only a few paces from the **Kindertransport** memorial, immediately above the exit from the Underground and more or less opposite Platform 7. On the memorial itself are well over a thousand names. Below it are two bronzes: on the left, a 1917 portrait roundel of **Captain Charles Fryatt [3]** by *H. T. H. van Golberdinge*; on the right, a 1923 portrait relief of **Field Marshal Sir Henry Wilson [4]** by *C. L. Hartwell*.

Everyone knows of Nurse Edith Cavell's fate in 1915 at the hands of the Germans; Fryatt was a less well-known victim the following year. As the captain of one of the Great Eastern Railway's ferries, which continued to ply between England and neutral Holland throughout the Great War, Fryatt had rammed and sunk a German submarine, *U-33*, which had patently been going to sink his own vessel. Fryatt was subsequently captured by the Germans, 'tried' as an alleged *franc-tireur* (or more accurately, as a civilian unlawfully taking up arms) and shot. His execution provoked worldwide outrage and was described by Asquith, the Prime Minister of the day, as murder. The service accompanying the re-interment of his remains in England after the war was attended by the King and Queen of the Belgians.

Wilson – Ulsterman, Francophile and francophone, staff officer and incorrigible intriguer – was Chief of the Imperial General Staff from 1918 to 1922. On giving up that office, he became an Ulster Unionist Member of Parliament, and a pretty outspoken one at that. On 22 July 1922 he unveiled the **War Memorial** at Liverpool Street. He was murdered by Fenians – as Irish republican terrorists were then known – two hours later upon his return to his home in Eaton Place.

Bishopsgate

Leave the station concourse on its east side and turn left and walk up the left-hand side of Bishopsgate. As you walk, on your right you will pass the junction with Brushfield Street, running away towards Commercial Road and the beginning of the East End. Admire at its far end the magnificent restored frontage of *Hawksmoor's* Christ Church, Spitalfields. Before you reach Primrose Street you will find the first of Broadgate's modern public sculptures, *Bruce McLean's* 1993 **Eye-I [5]**, an abstract steel structure in turquoise, mauve, blue, red and yellow. After a lot of contemplation, you may just be able to perceive the Hollywood-style female face that this work is supposed to resemble, with one eye open and the other covered by a mop of hair.

From **Eye-I** cut through to the north-east corner of Exchange Square, one of the three big open piazzas in Broadgate, spanning the entire width of Liverpool Street Station's tracks below. Here you find – you could not possibly miss it – the Columbian painter and sculptor *Fernando Botero's* monumental 1989 bronze **The Broadgate Venus [6]** (see illustration, page 100). It is a huge Venus, lying on her right side, with extremely voluptuous proportions, all 5 tons of them.

In the north-east corner of Exchange Square, at the foot of the steps down to Appold Street, is a work by Spain's premier living sculptor, *Xavier Corberó*. It is a curious granite group called **The Broad Family [7]**, of 1991; two adults, a child, a dog and perhaps a football. The highly abstract quality of the group means that you have to struggle towards that interpretation, the only figurative representation in the group being the barely visible feet and ankles of the child.

At the junction of Appold Street, Sun Street and Broad Lane, in the middle of the decahedral island roundabout, stand **Ganapathi and Devi [8]**, two colossal abstract representations of those two Hindu deities by *Stephen Cox* in black Indian granite, in 1988.

Pass through the gates on the south side of the island and re-enter Broadgate proper. Walk down into Broadgate Square, the outdoor hub (or perhaps hubbub, with its occasional open-air skating rink in the Broadgate Arena) of the whole development. In the south-east quadrant, extravagantly and implausibly airborne, is *Barry Flanagan's* 1988 bronze **Leaping Hare on Crescent and Bell [9]**. From the south side of the Circle, looking down towards Blomfield Street and into the Broadgate Octagon, you cannot miss *Richard Serra's* huge 1987 work in now deliberately rusted steel – five tall vertical steel plates forming **Fulcrum [10]**.

Leave the Circle via its north-west quadrant and walk into Broadgate's third large open space, Finsbury Avenue Square. In the south-west corner is *George Segal's* 1987 bronze group of six life-size figures – three men and three women – walking away from the entrance to the offices of UBS, which are at Number 1 Finsbury Avenue, immediately behind the group. The piece is entitled **Rush Hour [11]** (see illustration, right), but the group has more the look of a clutch of hard-pressed and disappointed debtors leaving a most unsatisfactory meeting with their bankers, or perhaps hard-pressed and disappointed bankers leaving their distressed bank.

Follow Finsbury Avenue down towards Eldon Street and on your right you will find **Bellerophon Taming Pegasus [12]**, *Jacques Lipchitz's* 1966 bronze, which previously stood in the north-west corner of Broadgate Square. The statue is cleverly poised on Bellerophon's legs and strongly conveys the violent efforts of Pegasus to escape, but otherwise it is a brutal and unlovely work to behold.

The Broadgate public sculpture is a curate's egg of a collection, ranging from the figurative to the highly abstract, from stone to steel, from visually pleasing through cryptically bland. But as a modern development that is otherwise seriously short of soft edges and embellishments, there can be little doubt that Broadgate greatly benefits from these sculptures. It is very much to the credit of all those involved, and particularly the developers, that despite the enormous expense of the entire scheme there were still sufficient funds and imaginative inspiration to commission this degree of artistic decoration.

Finsbury Circus

Leave Broadgate and move on to a mixture of old and new. Walk to the end of Finsbury Avenue, turn right into Eldon Street and then left into Blomfield Street. A short way along you will see

Finsbury Circus on your right, and the City's only open-air bowling green. Follow the Circus round to the north-west corner. Your specific interest is the Circus's single architectural masterpiece, *Lutyens'* Britannic House, with its frontages to both the Circus and Moorgate. Compare Britannic House with its more modern, bland and pedestrian neighbours round the north side of the Circus. In particular look at *Francis Derwent Wood's* 1924 statuary at second-floor level on the Circus frontage, depicting (from right to left) a **Woman and Baby**, **Persian Scarf Dancer**, **Turbaned Man Carrying Water** and **Britannia with Trident [13]**, this last being repeated in reverse on the Moorgate corner. At the south end of the Finsbury Circus frontage Britannic House still proudly displays the Royal Institute of British Architect's 1925 London Architecture Medal.

The next building down Moorgate from Britannic House, going towards London Wall, is **Electra House [14]**, originally the Edwardian headquarters of the Eastern Telegraph Company and now the home of London Metropolitan University. The most interesting aspect of the Moorgate facade is the number of distinguished sculptors who had a hand in its reliefs, friezes and other sculptural decoration: *George Frampton* (perhaps best remembered for **Peter Pan**, see page 20), *F. W. Pomeroy*, *William Goscombe John* and *Alfred Drury* for certain, and possibly also *Herbert Hampton* and *Charles Allen*. Figures receiving and transmitting messages, allegorical depictions of far-flung lands connected by the telegraph and the massive bronze globe on the roof, all firmly emphasize the telegraphic enterprise of the original occupant.

Guildhall and Around

Continue down Moorgate until you reach the junction with London Wall. Cross Moorgate and then cross London Wall and walk down into Coleman Street. You are heading for the Guildhall, but on the way down Coleman Street you pass *Antanas Brazdys's* 1969 piece entitled **Ritual [15]**, an abstract stainless-steel work, the prize-winning sculpture in a competition for British sculptors under the age of thirty-five.

Turn right into Mason's Avenue, cross Basinghall Street and you reach Guildhall Yard. On its east side is its newest building, *Richard Gilbert Scott's* Guildhall Art Gallery of 1999. Under the arcade at street level are four stone busts, all by *Tim Crawley*: from right to left, **Wren**, **Shakespeare**, **Cromwell** and **Pepys [16]**. Next to **Pepys** at the north end of the arcade, is a stone three-quarter relief of **Richard Whittington [17]** – Dick Whittington, the most famous of all the 682 lord mayors of London – and his cat, by *Lawrence Tindall* in 1999.

Leave Guildhall Yard on the opposite (west) side. Aldermanbury runs up the west side of the Guildhall complex, and at its junction with Love Lane there is a small formal garden, on the site of the old churchyard of St Mary Aldermanbury, which was destroyed in the Blitz. *Charles Allen's* 1896 bronze bust of **Shakespeare [18]**, on a pink granite plinth, is not in fact another memorial to the Bard, but rather is inscribed 'To the memory of John Heminge and Henry Condell, fellow actors and personal friends of Shakespeare ... to their disinterested affection the world owes all that it calls Shakespeare. They alone collected his dramatic writings regardless of pecuniary loss and without the hope of any profit gave them to the world. THEY THUS MERITED THE GRATITUDE OF MANKIND'. Heminge and Condell (who lived and were buried in this parish) were Shakespeare's partners at the Globe Theatre and were responsible for the publication of the *First Folio* in 1623.

On the east side of Love Lane, immediately to the north of the Guildhall, is the first of two works in quick succession by *Karin Jonzen*. **Towards Tomorrow [19]** is a 1972 pair of bronze nude figures, a reclining woman and a seated man, both looking up and away to the west. Turn right into Aldermanbury and walk through Aldermanbury Square to London Wall. You will find in Brewer's Hall Gardens her second work, **The Gardener [20]**, a 1971 roughly finished bronze of a kneeling, planting gardener on the south side of London Wall. On the east side of the gardens, climb the steps to Bassishaw High Walk, which crosses London Wall and takes you up to the south-east corner of the Barbican.

Barbican

We find first, in the bleak garden on the east side of St Alphage House, *Michael Ayrton's* 1973 bronze **Minotaur [21]**. It is a most explicitly endowed minotaur, bowed and resting on its left knee, but exuding menace. It has recently been moved from Postman's Park, which you will be visiting very shortly.

Walk across to the north side of the Barbican complex, in order to see the next three sculptures. The Barbican 'trio' are at the junction of the main north-south walkway and the bridge to the south-east entrance into the Arts Centre. *Matthew Spender's* **Barbican Muse [22]**, of 1994, is a reclining, well-endowed female figure in polyurethane and glass fibre, and lots of gold leaf, holding in her left hand the masks of tragedy and comedy and pointing to the entrance with her other hand. In Ben Jonson Place, on the north Barbican podium, are *John Ravera's* **Dolphin Fountain [23]** and *Charlotte Mayer's* **Ascent [24]**, both of 1990. The former is a blue-green bronze of two dolphins seemingly standing on their tails, the latter a spiralling formation of twenty-one steel poles.

At Alban Gate, on the podium under the huge office block, is *Ivan Klapez's* **Unity [25]**, a 1992 life-size bronze. Two nude dancers are engaged in an exuberant Latin American number.

The High Walk continues westwards to the Museum of London, where stand both *Christopher LeBrun's* 2001 bronze **Union – Horse with Two Discs [26]** and **The Aldersgate Flame [27]**. The latter, an abstract bronze flame erected in 1981, is the memorial to John Wesley's conversion place, marking as closely as possible the site in Nettleton Court (at the lower, street level) of Wesley's conversion experience in May 1738, which is generally regarded as marking the spiritual birth of Methodism and the world Methodist movement.

Follow Aldersgate south from the Museum of London roundabout, walking on the west (right-hand) side of the road. After 30 yards, on the south side of St Botolph Aldgate, you will find Postman's Park, which was laid out as a park in the 1880s and takes its name from the proximity of the former General Post Office in King Edward Street, on the west side of the park. Its principal point of interest is the **Loggia [28]**, which was first conceived by *G. F. Watts* in 1887 as a monument to mark Queen Victoria's Golden Jubilee and was finally completed in 1899. It shelters fifty-three glazed and decorated plaques commemorating what might be called ordinary people's acts of civic heroism, almost all chosen by Watts and (after his death in 1904) his widow. The plaques record 'heroic sacrifices' from 1863 to 1927. The earliest is perhaps the best of them all, commemorating 'Sarah Smith Pantomime Artiste at Prince's Theatre, Died of terrible injuries received when attempting in her inflammable dress to extinguish the flames which had enveloped her companion January 24 1863'. The intent of the overall

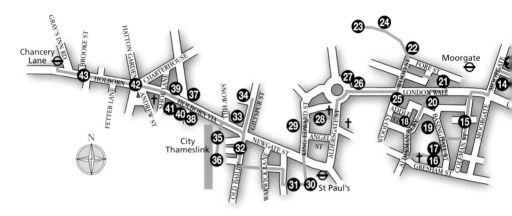

memorial was well meaning, even noble; the effect slightly quaint, even bathetic. *T. H. Wren's* 1905 wooden statuette of **Watts** himself has been temporarily removed from its niche halfway along the loggia by the City Surveyor for safekeeping.

Leave the park on its west side and cross King Edward Street. You will come to the former General Post Office – now little more than the facade of a much larger new office development which houses an American investment bank – and to the statue of **Sir Rowland Hill [29]** on the pavement before it. It is a bronze by *Edward Onslow Ford* in 1882, three years after Hill's death, which was originally erected outside the Royal Exchange and moved here in 1923. Educator and philanthropist, and the subject of two other public statues in Birmingham and his birthplace Kidderminster (the latter by *Thomas Brock*), Rowland Hill is principally remembered – and most justifiably so – as the father of Penny Post. This system is still in place today: of uniform rate, pre-paid inland postage with adhesive stamps and which replaced the Byzantine and fabulously expensive and inefficient postal arrangements that prevailed at the beginning of the Victorian era. In Gladstone's words, Hill's Penny Post 'had run like wildfire through the civilized world; never perhaps was a local invention (for such it was) and improvement applied in the lifetime of its author to the advantages of such vast multitudes of his fellow creatures'.

Paternoster Square

Walk southwards down King Edward Street, cross Newgate Street and enter the new Paternoster Square development. During the late 1980s and throughout the 1990s, this area was either a grim wasteland, as the previous 1960s *Holford* scheme became progressively untenanted, or a building site. Although there are strong and varying views on the architectural merits of the new scheme, it has undoubtedly revived and smartened the immediate northern environs of *Wren's* masterpiece, St Paul's Cathedral.

① Children of the Kindertransport
② Great Eastern Railway Great War Memorial
③ Captain Charles Fryatt
④ FM Sir Henry Wilson
⑤ Eye-I
⑥ Broadgate Venus
⑦ Broad Family
⑧ Ganapathi and Devi
⑨ Leaping Hare on Crescent and Bell
⑩ Fulcrum
⑪ Rush Hour
⑫ Bellerophon Taming Pegasus
⑬ Britannia with Trident
⑭ Electra House
⑮ Ritual
⑯ Pepys
⑰ Richard Whittington
⑱ Shakespeare
⑲ Towards Tomorrow
⑳ The Gardener
㉑ Minotaur
㉒ Barbican Muse

㉓ Dolphin Fountain
㉔ Ascent
㉕ Unity
㉖ Union – Horse with Two Discs
㉗ The Aldersgate Flame
㉘ Loggia
㉙ Sir Rowland Hill
㉚ Good Shepherd
㉛ Paternoster Square Column
㉜ Central Criminal Court
㉝ Charles Lamb
㉞ Golden Boy of Pye Corner
㉟ Echo
㊱ Zuni-Zennor
㊲ Science and Fine Art
㊳ Commerce and Agriculture
㊴ Sir Henry FitzAylwin
㊵ Sir Thomas Gresham
㊶ Walworth
㊷ Prince Albert
㊸ Royal Fusiliers War Memorial

On the east side of the large piazza that occupies the middle of the development is *Elisabeth Frink's* **Good Shepherd [30]** – an unmistakable *Frink* sculpture, with a typical and characteristically powerful head, of a shepherd preceded by five sheep. This was originally erected in 1975 in the bleak, windswept piazza of the previous *Holford* development. It was then briefly housed outside the Museum of London while the present scheme was built and was reinstated here in its rightful home in 2003.

Towards the left side of the piazza is the **Paternoster Square Column [31]**. Designed by *Whitfield Partners*, the lead architects for the overall development, the column is 23 metres (75 feet) high, and is the tallest free-standing monument to be erected in London since the nineteenth century. The shaft of the column comprises five 6-ton pieces of Portland stone, topped by a further 10-ton piece carved as a Corinthian capital, and crowned again by a 3-metre (10-foot) high copper urn that is illuminated at night. The whole column, which is based on a design by *Inigo Jones* for the west end of the cathedral, is mounted on a limestone and granite water feature with eight cascades – all usually waterless, of course.

Leave the piazza on its west side, cross Warwick Lane and Warwick Square, and follow Warwick Passage under the **Central Criminal Court [32]** into Old Bailey, from which the court takes its much better-known name. Note the gilded bronze figure of justice atop the dome and the Portland-stone group immediately above the old main entrance – the veiled figure of the recording angel and her supporting handmaidens bearing sword and looking-glass, representing Fortitude and Truth – both 'justice' and the stone group are the work of *F. W. Pomeroy* and date from the construction of the old main building in 1900–07.

Continue to the top of Old Bailey and cross at the traffic lights, over Holborn Viaduct, to the left side of Giltspur Street. Walk up the street and on your left is the east wall of the watch house of one of the most delightfully named City churches, St Sepulchre-without-Newgate. Here there is a bronze bust of **Charles Lamb [33]** by *William Reynolds-Stephens*, a 1935 work. The inscription on one plaque below reads: 'Perhaps the most loved name in English literature who was a Bluecoat boy here for seven years.' The bust is recorded by an additional plaque as having been 'Moved here in December 1962 from Christchurch Greyfriars in Newgate Street (bombed during the Second World War, and now a rose garden), which stands beside the former site of Charles Lamb's school Christ's Hospital.' Charles Lamb, the essayist, was a friend of both Coleridge and Wordsworth, and died in 1834. The memorial was proposed on the occasion of the centenary of his death. St Sepulchre also houses the ashes of Sir Henry Wood, the founder of the annual Promenade Concerts or 'Proms', and has stained glass windows commemorating Dame Nellie Melba, the Australian soprano, and Captain John Smith, whose statue is outside St Mary-le-Bow (see page 93). It is also the home of the bells of Old Bailey, of nursery rhyme fame.

Further up Giltspur Street, at first-floor level on the building at the junction with Cock Lane, is **The Golden Boy of Pye Corner [34]**, a small gilt boy of uncertain date and possibly by *Puckeridge*, with the inscription 'This Boy is in Memmory put up for the late Fire of London Occasioned by the Sin of Gluttony 1666' (for indeed the Great Fire began and ended with food, from Pudding Lane to Pye Corner). This spot marks the furthest extent westwards of the Great Fire. A separate contemporary plaque explains the boy's history: 'The Boy at Pye Corner was erected to commemorate the staying of the Great Fire which beginning at Pudding Lane was ascribed to the sin of gluttony when not attributed to the papists as on the Monument and the Boy was made prodigiously fat to enforce the moral. He was originally built into the front of a public house called "The Fortune of War" which used to occupy this site and was pulled down in 1910. "The Fortune of War" was the chief house of call north of the river for resurrectionists in body snatching days years ago. The landlord used to show the room where on benches round the walls the bodies were placed labelled with the snatchers' names waiting till the surgeons at St Bartholomew's could run round and appraise them.'

Holborn Viaduct

Retrace your steps to the junction with Holborn Viaduct. The name embraces the roadway from Newgate Street to Holborn Circus, and you could be forgiven for thinking of it today as a broad road with a bridge in the middle over Farringdon Street. The viaduct is in fact what its name implies, 425 metres (1,400 feet) of Victorian viaduct, with the bridge in the middle as its largest span.

Cross over the road and walk west for a few yards before turning left into Fleet Place for a brief diversion. A remarkable feat of railway engineering at the beginning of the 1990s resulted in the complete removal of the 1870s viaduct connecting Blackfriars and Holborn Viaduct stations. It was replaced by the new subterranean City Thameslink station, with the reopening at the same time of the old Snow Hill railway tunnel, London's only north-south 'through' railway service. The Luton to Brighton direct service now passes beneath where you are standing.

Stephen Cox's 1993 work in black Indian granite, **Echo [35]**, two opposed headless and semi-abstract torsos, stands a few paces down the street. A little further on, attached to the wall of 10 Fleet Place is **Zuni-Zennor [36]**, a twisting linear 1993 sculpture by *Eilis O'Connell*, in brass with a green patina. After viewing these, walk back to Holborn Viaduct, turn left and proceed westwards and on the bridge itself are four bronze statues, all of 1869. **Science** and **Fine Art [37]** on the north side, both by the sculpting firm of *Farmer & Brindley*, and **Commerce** and **Agriculture [38]** on the south side, both by *Henry Bursill*. The step-buildings at the south-west and south-east corners of the bridge date from the construction of the viaduct itself in the 1860s and niches in those buildings still support *Bursill's* original statues of **Sir Henry FitzAylwin [39]**, the first Lord Mayor of London, and **Sir Thomas Gresham [40]** (see page 97).

The corresponding step-buildings on the north side and their statues – **Sir William Walworth**, Lord Mayor and slayer of Wat Tyler, and **Sir Hugh Myddelton**, promoter of the New River scheme – were severely damaged during the Second World War. A copy of **Walworth [41]**, based on a photograph of *Bursill's* original plaster model, was placed above the rebuilt north-west steps in 2000, but Myddelton has to be content with his solitary statue above the **Royal Exchange** (see page 97).

Continue westwards, and in the middle of Holborn Circus you will find *Charles Bacon's* 1874 equestrian bronze of **Prince Albert [42]**. The Prince Consort, in field marshal's uniform, raises his hat in salute, an unusual gesture for a mounted officer in uniform but one which gives the statue greater warmth and informality. He is getting a little shabby, but is due for imminent restoration and a shift to a slightly more accessible island in High Holborn itself, rather than in the middle of Holborn Circus. At each end of the plinth is a seated bronze allegory – of **Peace** at the west end, with an olive crown, and of **History** at the other end, with her books. The north and south bronze reliefs show Albert with a ceremonial mallet beside the foundation stone of the new Royal Exchange, and Britannia enthroned, with a lion at her feet, holding out laurel crowns. Behind **Prince Albert**, at the north-west quadrant of the circus, there stood for many years Gamages department store, which was demolished as recently as 1974. To its west, on the other side of Leather Lane and very much still standing, is the colossal Victorian Gothic headquarters of Prudential Assurance.

Continue west along High Holborn, on the south side of the road. Outside the Prudential Assurance HQ, on the island in the middle of the carriageway, is the **Royal Fusiliers War Memorial [43]** (see illustration, right), with its 1922 bronze of a single fusilier by *Albert Toft*, commemorating the twenty-two thousand nameless Great War dead of the Royal Fusiliers (City of London Regiment), whose many battalions are listed on the plinth in stark and poignant remembrance.

Continue walking westwards and at the junction with Gray's Inn Road you will see Chancery Lane Underground Station.

11. BLOOMSBURY – FROM HIGH HOLBORN TO ST PANCRAS

START	Chancery Lane Underground Station (Central line)
FINISH	Kings Cross Underground Station (Victoria, Piccadilly, Northern (Bank branch), Hammersmith & City, Circle and Metropolitan lines)
DISTANCE	6.25 km (3.8 miles)
DURATION	1 ¾ hours

This walk begins on the western edge of the City, at the bottom of Gray's Inn Road, where Holborn runs into High Holborn. Street and district (the old Borough of Holborn embraced much of Bloomsbury and London University) derive their name from the Holbourne, the name given to the part of the River Fleet that runs down into the Thames on the west side of the City, more or less along the line of today's Farringdon Street. Holborn and High Holborn are the ancient western approach to the City, and even today they form the final stretch of the A40, which begins as far west as Fishguard in Wales. From Holborn, the walk wanders northwards through Bloomsbury, and ends with London's three great northern railway stations, Euston, St Pancras and King's Cross.

Gray's Inn

Take the 'northside' exit from Chancery Lane Tube Station and proceed west for 30 yards to the entrance to Gray's Inn, the most northerly and the least frequented of the four surviving Inns of Court, or quasi-collegiate legal institutions, which border the western side of the City and where the barristers, or court lawyers, have their chambers. Inner and Middle Temple and Lincoln's Inn are Gray's three fellow survivors, but street and building names still recall other long deceased Inns of Chancery such as Barnard's, Clement's, Clifford's and Furnival's, and the much grander Serjeants' Inn, whose eponymous denizens were immortalized by Dickens in *The Pickwick Papers*.

Enter Gray's Inn, and in South Square is *F. W. Pomeroy's* 1910 bronze of **Francis Bacon, Viscount St Albans [1]**, lawyer, politician, statesman, scientist, philosopher, intriguer and one of the greatest intellects of the Elizabethan and Jacobean age. Besides being successively Solicitor-General, Attorney-General, Lord Keeper (a legal office long defunct) and Lord Chancellor, Bacon was also Treasurer, or 'Chief Executive', of Gray's Inn from 1608 to 1617, and it was through that office that he left his most visible monument apart from his prodigious literary output, in the form of The Walks, a 2-hectare (5-acre) garden at the north end of the inn. The Walks are another of those remarkable oases of verdant tranquillity with which the centre of London is so blessed, and are a very pleasant diversion.

Between Two Inns

Retrace your steps back to High Holborn, turn right and immediately on your right and opposite the top of Chancery Lane you find the first of three works on this walk by *Eduardo*

Paolozzi, a 1987 bronze entitled **The Artist as Hephaistos** [2]. Both the sculpture and the postmodern building in whose ground-level niche it stands are rather brutal and discordant bedfellows for their immediate surroundings.

Lincoln's Inn Fields

Cross to the south side and continue walking up High Holborn, turning down Great Turnstile to reach the north-east corner of Lincoln's Inn Fields. At the bottom of Great Turnstile on the east side is Dolphin Court. Mounted at first-floor level is a graceful aluminium **Dolphin** [3], by *Annabel Richter Pentney* in 1989.

On the corner of the Fields themselves is an abstract metal cut-out entitled **Camdonian** [4], by *Barry Flanagan* in 1980, slightly reminiscent of an Alice in Wonderland playing card and not entirely in sympathetic step with most of the buildings around the Fields.

Lincoln's Inn Fields were developed rather earlier than some of the other West End squares featured in these walks, central London's urban development and sprawl having flowed progressively westward from its original heart, the City. From open, nondescript land at the turn of the seventeenth century, the Fields had become largely developed on the north, west and south sides by the middle of that century. Subsequent additions and replacements have resulted in no great architectural purity or consistency, although Sir John Soane's House and Museum in Numbers 12/14 on the north side are gems well worth visiting.

Just opposite the Soane Museum, on the north side of the Fields, is the memorial to **Margaret MacDonald** [5], the wife of Ramsay MacDonald, the first Labour Prime Minister. A bronze by *Richard Goulden*, unveiled in December 1914, surmounts a bench of grey Scottish granite and teak, commemorating a woman who was herself an active socialist and statistician before she died at the age of forty-one in 1911. She lived at Number 3 and, in the closing words of the lengthy eulogy on the back of the memorial, 'Took no rest from doing good'.

Red Lion Square

Leave the fields at the north-west corner and walk up Gate Street and Little Turnstile back to High Holborn. Cross the road to the right side of Procter Street, walk a short way before turning right into Red Lion Square to view two more recent radical memorials. At the far end of the square, half hidden in the rather untended greenery, is a bust of **Bertrand Russell, 3rd Earl Russell** [6], a 1979 bronze by *Marcelle Quinton*. Among the most distinguished of British twentieth-century philosophers, and arguably the most well-known, Russell is perhaps best remembered as one of the foremost campaigners for nuclear disarmament in the 1950s and 1960s. He also received the Order of Merit and was a Nobel Laureate.

At the west end of the square is *Ian Walters'* 1985 life-size bronze of **Fenner Brockway** [7]. The statue was unveiled by Michael Foot (then lately leader of the Labour Party) in the presence of its ninety-six-year-old subject, who died in 1988, six months short of his century. Socialist, anti-imperialist and peace campaigner, Brockway – as the 1996 supplement of the *ODNB* puts it – was born in the age of Gladstone and died in the age of Thatcher. The plinth is solemnly inscribed: 'In honour of his untiring efforts for peace and racial equality.' The statue itself strongly conveys the less solemn impression of someone emerging in a hurry from the bushes and trying to hail a taxi.

John Bunyan

Exit the square the same way you came in, turn left into Procter Street then right into Catton Street. Walk to the end of the street, to the junction with Southampton Row. There, in a first-floor niche above the former Baptist church, is *Richard Garbe's* 1901 stone statue of **John Bunyan [8]**, with the subscription of the opening words of his immortal masterpiece, *The Pilgrim's Progress*: 'As I walked through the wilderness of this world, I lighted on a certain place, where there was a Denn; and I laid me down in that place to sleep: and as I slept I dreamed a dream.'

St George's, Bloomsbury Way

Turn right into Southampton Row, walk a little way, then cross the road and turn left onto the south side of Bloomsbury Way. Follow the road until you come to **St George's Bloomsbury Way [9]**. The church was designed by *Nicholas Hawksmoor*. It was begun in 1716 and completed in 1731, and is described by Pevsner as 'perhaps the most grandiose of all London's eighteenth-century churches'. Look up at its unusual spire, which is stepped in accordance with Pliny's description of one of the Seven Wonders of the World: the mausoleum at Halicarnassus ordered for himself by the eponymous Mausolus, King of Caria, and erected by his queen, Artemisia, after his death in 353 BC.

Note the even more unusual statue of **George I** that surmounts the spire, in Roman dress and topped by a very obvious lightning conductor. At the base of the spire are perhaps the most informal stone sculpted depictions of the customary **Royal Supporters** – two pairs of lion-and-unicorn, with delightfully playful upside-down lions, and unicorns casually lying on the spire, each with a gleaming golden horn. It is not so much an unusual statue of George I as the only surviving one in London, neglect and vandalism having overwhelmed its counterpart in Leicester Square by the middle of the nineteenth century. The statue of **George I** is original and probably by the hand of one *Edward Strong*, a mason who may also have been responsible for the original lions and unicorns and the accompanying festoons and crowns. The original lions and unicorns were removed in 1871, probably on account of dilapidation, but a prodigious feat of restoration, notably aided by the stonemasonry of *Tim Crawley*, has resulted in the replacement of both pairs, as recently as May 2006.

Congress House

Continue to the end of Bloomsbury then cross the road and proceed up the west side of Museum Street. At the top, head west to the extension of Great Russell Street, on the other side of Bloomsbury Street. Just past the left turn to Dyott Street is Congress House (the Trades Union Congress Memorial Building), where there is a memorial that is an exception to this book's requirement of public accessibility. The open inner courtyard can only be reached through the main reception area, but *Jacob Epstein's* 1956 stone **Pietà [10]** – the TUC's war memorial – merits the exception, even if the original green marble background has subsequently been replaced by less dramatic mosaic tiles. The bronze **Spirit of Brotherhood [11]** by *Bernard Meadows* over the front entrance is a more mundane reflection of trade union solidarity.

British Museum

As you return along Great Russell Street, the view to the north is of the main, south facade of the **British Museum [12]**, *Robert Smirke's* monumental building of 1823–52, housing the first European public museum with a collection that was accepted as a national responsibility. Look

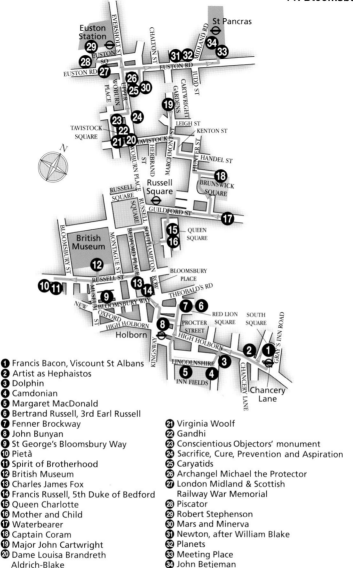

❶ Francis Bacon, Viscount St Albans
❷ Artist as Hephaistos
❸ Dolphin
❹ Camdonian
❺ Margaret MacDonald
❻ Bertrand Russell, 3rd Earl Russell
❼ Fenner Brockway
❽ John Bunyan
❾ St George's Bloomsbury Way
❿ Pietà
⓫ Spirit of Brotherhood
⓬ British Museum
⓭ Charles James Fox
⓮ Francis Russell, 5th Duke of Bedford
⓯ Queen Charlotte
⓰ Mother and Child
⓱ Waterbearer
⓲ Captain Coram
⓳ Major John Cartwright
⓴ Dame Louisa Brandreth
   Aldrich-Blake

㉑ Virginia Woolf
㉒ Gandhi
㉓ Conscientious Objectors' monument
㉔ Sacrifice, Cure, Prevention and Aspiration
㉕ Caryatids
㉖ Archangel Michael the Protector
㉗ London Midland & Scottish
   Railway War Memorial
㉘ Piscator
㉙ Robert Stephenson
㉚ Mars and Minerva
㉛ Newton, after William Blake
㉜ Planets
㉝ Meeting Place
㉞ John Betjeman

at the group of sculpted figures in the pediment: these, from left to right, illustrate the progress of civilization and form the last major work by *Richard Westmacott*, who was also the sculptor of the next two statues that you will see.

A Pair of Whigs

Return to Great Russell Street, cross over the road and walk up to Bloomsbury Square. Large parts of Bloomsbury were owned by the Dukes of Bedford and successive Dukes in the late eighteenth and early nineteenth centuries were prominent Whig grandees. Therefore it is appropriate that one of the most famous of all Whig politicians, **Charles James Fox [13]** (1749–1806), should have his statue on the north side of Bloomsbury Square, facing up Bedford Place towards Russell Square. It is an 1816 posthumous bronze of a seated Fox in Roman dress, holding a copy of Magna Carta. A pre-eminent parliamentarian, a sympathizer with both the American and the French revolutions, twice Foreign Secretary (albeit at each end of Pitt the Younger's prodigious tenure of office as Prime Minister), nevertheless Fox's libertarian and libertine tendencies, his espousal of the dissolute Prince of Wales and the consequent constant enmity of George III all made for a political career of rather less substance and success than the reputation with which his name is associated.

Cross over Bloomsbury Place and walk up Bedford Place to Russell Square. Looking back towards **Fox** down Bedford Place is **Francis Russell, 5th Duke of Bedford [14]**, an 1809 bronze of the Duke, who died in 1802. The Duke oversaw the building of a great part of Bloomsbury, as is commemorated by the frequent appearance of the names Bedford, Russell, Woburn and Tavistock, in streets and squares. Besides being a prominent Whig, the Duke was also an agriculturalist. The right hand of the statue rests on a ploughshare, there are agricultural scenes depicted on both side reliefs of the plinth and the ducal ermine is worn, a little incongruously, over classical rustic vestments.

Queen's Square Gardens

As you leave Russell Square at its south-east corner, a small nineteenth-century bronze plaque records that the house formerly on this site was the home of Sir Thomas Lawrence, President of the Royal Academy. A short walk back down Southampton Row and left through Cosmo Place brings you to Queen's Square Gardens and a fine and rare example of lead statuary at the north end of the central

garden. That the subject of the statue is a queen is unarguable – but which one? Having been thought at various times to be each of Mary (co-regnant, and wife of William III), Anne (also regnant) and Caroline (consort of George II), the statue is now expressly labelled: 'This statue, thought in the 19th century to be of Queen Anne, is now widely regarded as that erected in April 1775 to commemorate **Queen Charlotte [15]**, (see illustration, left) consort of King George III.' The sculptor is unknown, which is a pity because this is a fine depiction of an attractive woman with exquisite working on her brocaded dress.

Facing **Queen Charlotte**, in the middle of the gardens, is a little half-torso and head of a **Mother and Child [16]**, a 2001 bronze by *Patricia Finch*. Also note the small statue in the niche at first-floor level of St John's House, Number 12, by an unknown hand but possibly of **St John**. The greater part of the other buildings around the square today forms part of the National Hospital for Neurology and Neurosurgery.

Around Coram's Fields

Leave the square at the north end, turn right and walk along Guilford Street until you come to Guilford Place, opposite the south gateway into Coram's Fields. Here you find **The Waterbearer [17]**, once again by an unknown hand, a stone sculpture of a girl with a water pitcher.

Cross over Guilford Place and enter Coram's Fields through the south gateway and walk to the north side of Brunswick Square. You will find The Foundling Museum, a 1930s neo-Georgian building on the site of the former Foundling Hospital, which was demolished in 1926 when the hospital moved out of London, briefly to Redhill and then to Berkhamsted. Captain Thomas Coram founded the hospital in 1739, after seventeen years of efforts to do so and in the teeth of considerable opposition. The 'foundlings' were the thousands of babies and young children, almost all illegitimate, who were simply abandoned on the streets of London in the early eighteenth century. The opposition to Coram's plan was the deeply entrenched prejudice against the notion of giving any sort of comfort or relief to illegitimacy. Coram, however, was a man of extraordinary vision, conviction and determination, and he persisted in his philanthropic campaign to establish – as his eventual Royal Charter of 17 October 1739 described it – a hospital for the 'Education and Maintenance of Exposed and Deserted Young Children'.

Besides being a home and hostel for young children, the hospital was also a cultural centre: during the last ten years of his life before his death in 1759, Handel conducted or attended an annual performance of his *Messiah* in the chapel; Hogarth and Rysbrack were among the first governors, and they and Gainsborough, Reynolds and Ramsay were among many leading artists of the day who gave their works to the hospital in order to raise funds. In fact, their annual exhibitions were the direct precursors of the annual exhibitions (and led to the establishment) of the Royal Academy, of which Reynolds was to become the first President.

Outside the museum is *William McMillan's* 1963 bronze of a seated **Captain Coram [18]** (see illustration, right) holding his charter in his right hand. This replaced *William Calder Marshall's* 1851 statue, which moved with the hospital to Berkhamsted. Nothing remains of the original grand hospital buildings, but the saved and restored interiors and fittings that are housed in the museum, the statue and the name of the adjoining fields together make an enduring memorial to this remarkable pioneer in the cause of child welfare.

Cartwright Gardens

Leave the north-west corner of the square, turn right into Hunter Street, left into Handel Street and right into Kenton Street up to the junction with Tavistock Place. Turn left into Tavistock Place, then turn right, crossing the road into Marchmont Street. Walk up the street into Cartwright Gardens. *George Clarke's* 1831 bronze of **Major John Cartwright [19]**, the veteran late eighteenth- and early nineteenth-century radical and, in particular, advocate of universal suffrage, is unexceptional, but the subscription is sufficiently extraordinary to merit quoting in full: 'The Firm Consistent Persevering Advocate of "Universal Suffrage Equal Representation Vote by Ballot and Annual Parliaments" He was the first English writer who openly maintained the independence of the United States of America and although his distinguished merits as a Naval Officer [he spent ten years in the Navy before acquiring his Majority in the Militia] in 1776 presented the most flattering prospects of professional advancement, yet he nobly refused to draw his sword against the rising liberties of an oppressed and struggling people. In grateful commemoration of his inflexible integrity, exalted patriotism, "profound constitutional knowledge" and in sincere admiration of the unblemished virtues of his private life This statue was erected by public subscription near the spot where he closed his useful and meritorious career.' Perhaps a touch of hyperbole you might think, but not so, according to the *ODNB*, which describes Cartwright as 'one of the most generous-minded public men of his time ... tender to his opponents, forgiving to detractors, and always open-handed'. The statue was erected here because Cartwright spent the last years of his life living in Burton Crescent, as the west side of Cartwright Gardens used to be known.

Tavistock Square

Walk back down Marchmont Street to the junction. Turn right into Tavistock Place and walk to Tavistock Square (the Marquessate of Tavistock is the second title of the Duke of Bedford, and the courtesy title of his heir). In the south-east corner is an unusual bronze double bust, back to back, of **Dame Louisa Brandreth Aldrich-Blake [20]**. The bronzes are by *A. G. Walker*, the seat and base by *Edwin Lutyens*. Dame Louisa, later an eminent surgeon, has the interesting accolade from the *ODNB* of being described while at school as 'silent but not unsociable, and distinguished for her skill in boxing and cricket, at that date [the 1880s] unusual in a girl'.

In the south-west corner is a bronze bust of **Virginia Woolf [21]**, who lived in a house (now demolished) on the south side of the square between 1924 and 1939. This is where most of her greater novels were written. The bust was erected by the Virginia Woolf Society of Great Britain in 2004.

In the middle of the square is *Fredda Brilliant's* 1968 bronze statue of **Gandhi [22]**. The Mahatma – properly, Mohandas Karamchand Gandhi – was assassinated by a Hindu fanatic in 1948, but not before he had seen the birth of the post-Raj independent India of which he is widely held to be the spiritual father. The statue is clad in Gandhi's characteristic fakir's attire, and was unveiled by Harold Wilson, the Prime Minister, in May 1968.

In the north-west corner is a large **lump of slate [23]** (reminiscent of the Norwegian Navy Memorial in Hyde Park, see page 19) inscribed with the words 'To all those who have established and are maintaining the right to refuse to kill'. The stone was dedicated on 15 May 1994, International Conscientious Objectors Day.

On the east side of the square is *Lutyens'* headquarters building for the British Medical Association (BMA). You cannot go beyond the gates, but you can look into the courtyard. The gates themselves, by *Lutyens*, commemorate medical officers killed in the Great War. In the courtyard, the four large statues round the pool, by *James Woodford* and *S. Rowland Pierce*, representing **Sacrifice, Cure, Prevention** and **Aspiration [24]**, form the BMA's 1954 memorial to the Second World War.

There is a slate memorial plaque attached to the railings of the BMA that lists the names of the victims of the bus bomb that exploded in the square on 7 July 2005.

St Pancras New Church

Leave the square and walk on the right-hand side up to the top of Upper Woburn Place. At its junction with Euston Road is St Pancras New Church. Built in 1819–22, it is London's earliest church in a pure neo-Grecian style: from its six-column portico on the west side with fluted Ionic columns, to the feature that is of principal interest to you, the two smaller porticos on the north and south sides, towards the east end, with their duplicated versions of the caryatids of the Erechtheum on the Acropolis in Athens. These **caryatids [25]** – more decently attired than their Athenian elder sisters – are made of terracotta over an iron core, and were modelled by *J. C. F. Rossi,* who also has the unusual distinction of having fathered eight children by each of his two wives.

In the churchyard on the south side is a head (that may be familiar if you have seen the head on page 88) by *Emily Young,* representing **Archangel Michael the Protector [26].** Sculpted by her in 2004 it was subsequently erected and dedicated here with the inscriptions: 'In memory of the victims of the 7 July 2005 bombings and all victims of violence' and 'I will lift up mine eyes unto the hills'.

Euston Station

Diametrically opposite St Pancras New Church, on this busy crossroads, is Euston Station. Euston was the first of the major London railway termini, dating back to the 1830s and was the southern end of Robert Stephenson's London and Birmingham Railway. It was the site of the famous Greek Doric Euston Arch and some fine Victorian railway buildings, all of which were demolished in the 1960s in an act of architectural vandalism which, in the case of the arch, was possibly second only in twentieth-century London to the destruction of Sir John Soane's Bank of England in the 1920s. Euston today looks more like a tatty airport terminal than a grand railway station, but its southern approaches boast a statue, a sculpture and a monument.

Cross over Euston Road and into Euston Square. The monument is the **London Midland & Scottish Railway War Memorial [27]** to the dead of both world wars, which stands in Euston Grove, just off Euston Road. This is a 1921 work by *Reginald Wynn Owen,* with a stone obelisk guarded at its four corners by soldiers with heads bowed and rifles reversed.

The sculpture on the forecourt between the war memorial and the station is the second of the three works by *Eduardo Paolozzi* on this walk – **Piscator [28],** of 1980, an abstract work.

The statue of **Robert Stephenson [29],** an 1871 bronze by *Carlo Marochetti,* was originally erected in Euston Square but was moved to Euston Station in 1968. It has recently been moved again and now stands just outside the main pedestrian entrance to the station concourse. Robert was the son of George, who was the 'father' of steam locomotion and creator of the first and most famous of all railway engines, the 'Rocket', although Robert was involved in much of the Rocket's design. Robert himself was one of the two greatest Victorian railway engineers, Brunel being the other. Arguably Robert was the greater of the two, since his railway lines covered more of the country than Brunel's and it is his gauge, rather than Brunel's preferred original broad gauge on the Great Western Railway, which has prevailed as the universal global norm. In his later life Robert was also a Member of Parliament and an international railway consultant. He died on 12 October 1859, less than a month after his great rival, Brunel.

Duke's Road Diversion

You have two more main sites to visit, both further east along Euston Road, but you are going to make a quick diversion. Leave the Euston Station complex, turn left down Euston Road, then cross over into Duke's Road. Look at the interesting Grecian frontages and curved shop windows by *Thomas Cubitt*, built at much the same time as St Pancras New Church, and the later, Victorian drill hall, now The Place Theatre, with its attractive terracotta front and a medallion of **Mars and Minerva [30]** by *Thomas Brock*.

British Library

Retrace your steps back to the north side of Euston Road and walk eastwards to The British Library. The library, by *Colin St John Wilson*, was arguably the most important public building of the later twentieth century, certainly in London, perhaps in Britain. The end result of its protracted gestation over the last quarter of that century has been the formal separation of the library from the British Museum, of which it was formerly an integral part, and the creation of a new national home for Britain's written matter. It is a tribute to the success of the building that it is no Cinderella to its immediate neighbour to the east, *George Gilbert Scott's* High Victorian Gothic masterpiece, St Pancras Station and the Midland Grand Hotel, both of which you will see shortly.

You will find two works in the forecourt of the Library. Firstly, the third work by *Eduardo Paolozzi*, a large, brutal **Newton, after William Blake [31]**, of 1995. The pose is familiar from Blake's famous picture, but he is depicted here in familiar Paolozzi style as a semi-robotized man with bolted joints.

In the little circular arena in the south-east corner of the forecourt is *Antony Gormley's* **Planets [32]** of 2002. The work is eight (the sculptor evidently anticipating the subsequent recent downgrading of the former ninth planet, Pluto, to mere solar asteroid status) roughly cut lumps of granite, which may perhaps inspire planetary visions in the more imaginatively discerning eye.

St Pancras

Walk back to the Euston Road and head eastwards to St Pancras. The Midland Grand Hotel is itself still in builders' hands, in the course of its rescue and restoration as the grandest of hotels (with some exotic penthouse flats thrown in), after years of unused neglect. It is extraordinary that, although the derelict hotel was listed Grade 1 in 1967, it was only ten years later that British Rail finally accepted that demolition was not an option. The hotel is due to open in spring 2011.

The station's rescue, however, has now been perfected. St Pancras has replaced Waterloo as the terminus for the international Eurostar service and *William Barlow's* 1860s train shed – described by Pevsner as 'one of the outstanding examples of Victorian functionalism and daring' has been restored not only to its original architectural glory but also to its original and functional use.

Under the canopy of Barlow's engine shed, covering the station's main platforms, you find the last two statues on this walk. Both were commissioned for the renewed station, both figurative, both by distinguished modern sculptors and both installed just before the station reopened in 2007. The first is *Paul Day's* **The Meeting Place [33]**, a 9-metre (30-foot) high bronze couple, in a meeting 'clinch', immediately under the main station clock at the hotel end of the train shed. It jars horribly with the sumptuous splendour of its surroundings. The second is a sublime tribute to the man who did as much as any other individual to save St Pancras from the demolition contractor's ball

and chain. *Martin Jennings'* bronze representation of **John Betjeman [34]** (see illustration, above), Poet Laureate and architectural rescue crusader, is a fine work of sculpture. It is well sited, completely sympathetic to its environment, entirely characteristic and very 'Betjeman'. You can almost hear him looking up and saying 'My word!'

There are many entrances to King's Cross Underground Station within St Pancras Station.

12. PIMLICO AND CHELSEA EMBANKMENTS – FROM TATE GALLERY TO CHELSEA HARBOUR

START   Pimlico Underground Station (Victoria line)

FINISH   Battersea Bridge

DISTANCE   4.75 km (3 miles)

DURATION   1 ½ hours

Pimlico can sometimes seem like a sort of 'no man's land', separating its grander and very diverse neighbours – Westminster proper to the east, Belgravia to the north and Chelsea to the west. It shares the swank SW1 postcode of Belgravia, St James's and Victoria, but is the Cinderella of its postal siblings. It may have been largely the creation of Thomas Cubitt, and so is a substantial monument to that great Victorian developer, but nowadays the name 'Pimlico' is more likely to evoke visions of cheap hotels, the faded splendour of stucco Italianate terraces that have seen better days and large swathes of post-war public housing. Nevertheless, it is Pimlico where this walk begins, before broadly following the north bank upriver to Chelsea Harbour, with a few diversions on the way.

Tate Britain

Pimlico Underground Station is of modest interest in itself as the newest of the deep Underground stations (it was opened in 1972) until the construction of the Jubilee line extension to Canary Wharf and beyond. Take the 'Bessborough Street/Tate Britain' exit. You emerge into Bessborough Street. Follow the signs for Tate Britain, although you may care to notice an immediate work of public sculpture on your left in the form of the **Air Vent [1]** for the Underground, sculpted by *Eduardo Paolozzi* in 1982. It is a square tower structure, the upper part composed of vents, grills and pipes, while the lower part comprises twenty-eight relief panels depicting, quite literally, the nuts and bolts of the Industrial Age. From a distance, you get the impression of a 'heavy metal' Heath Robinson sketch, but without the essential Heath Robinson humour.

Follow the well-signposted route to Tate Britain. The Tate – strictly Tate Britain nowadays, to distinguish it from Tate Modern at Bankside and the Tate offspring at St Ives and Liverpool – was opened in 1897 as Sir Henry Tate's gift of a national gallery for British art, on part of the site of the then recently demolished Millbank Penitentiary (more of which in a moment). After several extensions and the acquisition of foreign modern art, the opening of both the Clore Gallery and Tate Modern has enabled Tate Britain to revert to its original primary role. It is therefore appropriate that *Thomas Brock's* 1904 bronze of **Sir John Everett Millais [2]** (see illustration, right) now stands outside the inshore end of the gallery, at the corner of Atterbury and John Islip Streets. With Holman Hunt and Dante Gabriel Rossetti (you will meet the latter again on this walk), Millais was one of the founders of the Pre-Raphaelite Brotherhood, that quintessentially Victorian Pre-Impressionist genre of painting. He was also artistically popular and very successful, receiving a baronetcy from Gladstone and succeeding Lord Leighton as President of the Royal Academy in 1896, only to die of throat cancer in the same year.

You could succumb to any number of diversions inside the Tate, including a very good lunch in the restaurant while enjoying *Rex Whistler's* splendid 1926 mural, *The Expedition in Pursuit of Rare Meats.* However, to continue on the walk, follow the shrapnel-scarred Atterbury Street frontage round to the front of the gallery and you find two bronze sculpture groups. To the right of the main entrance is *Henry C. Fehr's* **The Rescue of Andromeda [3]**, an 1893 work. The naked Andromeda, horror etched on her face, lies chained to a rock, under the widespread wings of a draconian sea-monster; but help is at hand in the guise of Perseus, conveniently passing by, having dispatched Medea and cut off her head; immediately falling in love with Andromeda, he stands poised above the monster, cleaver and petrifying Medean head ready to hand.

To the left of the entrance is *Charles Lawes-Wittewronge's* **The Death of Dirce [4]**, a 1908 smaller replica of an original 1906 marble. Dirce, the victim of another complicated mythological massacre, was tied to the horns of a bull by Amphion and Zethus (the characters are helpfully labelled in Greek script on the bronze). *Lawes,* who added the '*Wittewronge*' late in life in honour of an eighteenth-century forebear, was a prodigious Corinthian athlete and also the perpetrator of the libel that led to the protracted and ultimately successful court action by *Richard Belt* (see page 17).

Millbank

Leave Tate Britain, and cross to the river embankment. Proceeding upriver, and passing the Chelsea College of Art and Design (the former Royal Army Medical College), you find at the beginning of the next terrace **Jeté [5]**, a 1975 bronze by *Enzo Plazzotta.* It is a bronze dancer, based on the Royal Ballet's David Wall, in flamboyant mid-leap, with the sculpture cleverly balanced on the flowing sash trailing from the dancer's waist. More or less opposite on the other side of the road, by the embankment wall, a cylindrical **Mooring Stone [6]** carries a bronze plaque recording that this was the site of the Millbank Penitentiary from 1816 until

121

1890. The penitentiary, whose architect was *Robert Smirke* (also the architect of the British Museum, see page 112), was until 1867 the point of embarkation for prisoners sentenced to transportation to Australia.

A few yards on stands **Locking Piece [7]**, a 1964 work by *Henry Moore*, first located here in 1968. It is a monumental bronze of – as its name suggests – two locking pieces which, in the words of the helpful accompanying text, 'explores the relationship of two separate elements being put together and turned to look like a puzzle or joint'.

Vauxhall Bridge and Beyond

Continue walking to Vauxhall Bridge. The present **Vauxhall Bridge [8]** was built in the decade spanning 1900, replacing an earlier Regency iron bridge. Its interest on this walk lies in its ornamentation: the four steel piers supporting the five spans of the bridge are masked by tall bronze female figures. The four figures on the downstream side are by *Alfred Drury*, while the upstream counterparts are the work of *F. W. Pomeroy*.

There is a good view from the little-frequented Crown Reach Riverside Walk (follow the Thames Path signs), both of the upstream side of the bridge and of the vast St George Wharf residential development on the opposite bank, with its five futuristic 'winged' blocks hinting at a row of wimpled nuns.

Halfway along the riverside walk stands **River Cut Tide [9]**, a marble sculpture by *Paul Mason* in 2002. It is a strange abstract work: a short, irregular-scored and grooved white column.

At the upstream end of Crown Reach Riverside Walk you reach Pimlico Gardens and *John Gibson's* 1836 marble of **William Huskisson [10]**, a pensive figure in a toga. Present at the Fall of the Bastille in 1789, subsequently a Tory statesman and in and out of public office for over thirty years, Huskisson could fairly be said to have achieved less in life than his promise presaged, but to have achieved immortality by the manner of his death. He was the first fatal victim of a railway accident, when he was run over by a train at the opening of the Manchester and Liverpool Railway on 15 September 1830. The statue, by contrast, has come down in the world, having moved in 1915 to its present rather obscure site from the more illustrious surroundings of the **Royal Exchange**.

At the other end of these small gardens, outside the Westminster Boating Base, you find **The Helmsman [11]**, a 1996 bronze by *Andrew Wallace*. Perched on a slender pole, this is an abstract boat, slightly reminiscent of the bobbing barque of the BBC's cartoon Captain Pugwash nearly half a century ago, with a disproportionately large rudder and a strangely rigid – and naked – helmsman wearing a futuristic visored helmet.

Admire the Views

From Pimlico Gardens, you make the longest sculpture-free hike in all of the walks in this book. Leave the gardens on their inshore side, and turn left into Grosvenor Road. You pass by the end of Dolphin Square, the largest self-contained block of flats in Europe when built in the 1930s and even now evoking ancient naval glories, with its several houses named after Raleigh, Drake, Nelson, Howard, Beatty, Duncan, Rodney and the like. You will also pass the unloved and stark skeleton of the former Battersea Power Station on the opposite bank, now decommissioned for nearly a quarter of a century, but in its day the architectural benchmark for British power stations. As the river bends away to the left, there is a lovely view up the length of Chelsea Reach, beyond Battersea Bridge to Chelsea Harbour in the distance.

Walk under Grosvenor Railway Bridge, which feeds Victoria Station, and past the faded Second Empire splendour of Thames Water's Western Pumping Station – part of *Joseph Bazalgette's* remarkable sewerage system – and its attendant slender tower, more reminiscent of an Italian campanile.

Chelsea Bridge

On to Chelsea Bridge, and at the north-west corner of the crossroads you find the **Memorial to the VI. Dragoon Guards (The Carabiniers) in the South African War of 1899–1902 [12]**, erected in 1905, with its principal bronze relief by *Adrian Jones*. The two side panels list the names of the regiment's dead: thirty killed in action, and forty-seven died of wounds or disease. The central panel displays *Jones's* usual sureness of equine touch, with its representation of mounted and dismounted carabiniers going into action.

Royal Hospital

Proceed westwards along the Embankment, on the inshore pavement, and on your right you come to the Bullring Gate into the grounds of the Royal Hospital. Here you leave the river briefly for a sally as far afield as Sloane Square. Founded by Charles II in 1682, continued by his brother James II and completed by William and Mary in 1692, the Royal Hospital has provided a home for retired and invalided soldiers ever since, as the Latin inscription over the central colonnade records: '*In subsidium et levamen emeritorum senio belloque fractorum condidit Carolus Secundus auxit Jacobus Secundus perfecere Gulielmus et Maria Rex et Regina Anno Domini MDCXCII*'. With less grandeur but more homeliness than its conceptual inspiration, the Hôtel des Invalides in Paris that was founded by Louis XIV only a dozen years earlier, the Royal Hospital is one of *Christopher Wren's* secular masterpieces.

In the middle of the open grounds on the Embankment side stands the **Chilianwalla Monument [13]**, a granite obelisk erected in 1853 'to the memory of the 255 officers and NCO's and privates of the XXIV Regiment who fell at Chilianwalla on 13 January 1849' during the Second Anglo-Sikh War. All 255 names are engraved on the four sides of the obelisk. A supposedly well-equipped British force under General Lord Gough was bested by its Sikh opponents and unease at home about the serious casualty rate (shades of modern-day Afghanistan) caused Gough to be superseded as Commander-in-Chief by General Sir Charles Napier, the conqueror of Sind (see page 61) – although Gough brought the war to a successful conclusion by his later victory at the Battle of Goojesat before Napier could assume command. The damage to British prestige contributed to the political climate that led to the Indian Mutiny, although Gough himself still managed to go on and become both a viscount and a field marshal.

In the centre of the Main Court you see the founder, **Charles II [14]**, a bronze statue on a short cylindrical plinth, now restored to its original gilded state and positively dazzling to the eye. Like the more or less contemporary statue of **James II** in Trafalgar Square (see page 62), the monarch is in imperial Roman military attire. Although the plinth bears the name of *Grinling Gibbons* as sculptor, the statue is probably the work of *Arnold Quellin*, who worked in Gibbons' studio. Gibbons' pre-eminence lay in wood – for marble and bronze he wisely engaged others of greater expertise than his own, such as Quellin, who came from a distinguished Dutch sculpting family. For the Founder's Day Parade on 9 June every year, the statue is swathed with oak branches in commemoration of Charles's escape after the Battle of Worcester in September 1651, the final battle of the English Civil War, and his legendary concealment in an oak tree. The 'royal oak' is widely celebrated, from country pubs to successive warships of the Royal Navy, the last of which was sunk by a German U-boat in Scapa Flow in 1939.

Pass through the central block, between the Hall and the Chapel, and the oak motif is repeated outside the (north side) front of the hospital, where *Philip Jackson's* **Chelsea In-Pensioner [15]** (see illustration, below), a bronze of 2000, stands on a low, stone, cylindrical plinth, in frock coat and tricorn hat, with a raised stick in his right hand and an oak branch in his left, and a pile of spent ordnance at his feet. Around his plinth is the traditional soldier's prayer: 'O Lord you know how occupied I shall be this day If I forget thee Do not forget me.'

King's Road and Sloane Square

Upon leaving the hospital, turn right on to Royal Hospital Road. Immediately past Burton's Court, cross over into Franklin's Row. This road follows into Cheltenham Terrace. At the junction turn right on to King's Road. Just down on your right you will come to Duke of York

Square, the new piazza between the old Duke of York's Barracks and King's Road. In it stands *Simon Smith's* new (2007) stone statue of **Sir Hans Sloane [16]**, in full-bottomed wig and formal academic robes. This is yet another copy of *John Michael Rysbrack's* original alabaster work of 1737, which was commissioned by the Society of Apothecaries and erected in the Physic Garden. The original was moved to the British Museum in 1983, on account of its advanced state of deterioration, and was replaced by a carefully distressed fibreglass copy. That copy, however, developed holes, and was even possessed by a swarm of bees, and was replaced in the Physic Garden by a second copy, in jesmonite, an artificial mixture of resin and stone. The first copy then stood for a time at the west end of Sloane Square, facing Peter Jones department store, but has effectively been replaced by *Smith's* new copy, with its much clearer depiction of Sloane's powerful, but also benign, face.

As you continue towards Sloane Square, in the pedestrian passageway opposite Cadogan Gardens and Peter Jones, there are two small bronzes, **Two Pupils of** *c.* **1814 [17]** from the Royal Military Asylum that occupied the site from 1803 to 1909, when the Duke of York's Military School relocated to Dover. They are the work of *Allister Bowrell* in 2002. The girl is seated demurely on a low rectangular plinth; the boy is leapfrogging an 1819 iron bollard.

Continue down Kings Road, cross over Lower Sloane Street and then cross left into Sloane Square itself. In the centre of the square is **Venus Fountain [18]** (see illustration, above); a bronze by *Gilbert Ledward* (1953) of a naked kneeling nymph (or goddess – take your choice) with two pitchers, with water spilling from the larger and spouting from the smaller. The nymph is on a small round base that itself is set in and slightly above a large ornamental bronze urn, all in the middle of an octagonal basin.

Towards the Royal Court Theatre stands the stone **War Memorial [19]** to 'the men and women of Chelsea who gave their lives' in both world wars. It is a standard *Reginald Blomfield* war memorial cross above an octagonal stepped plinth bearing the subscription: 'Their lives for their

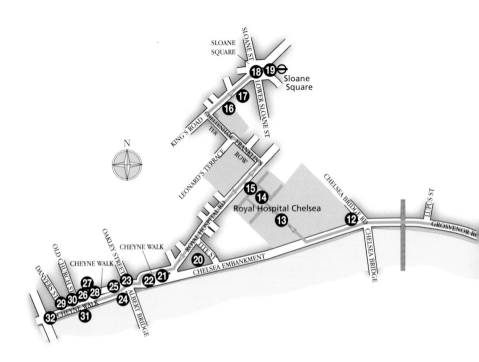

country, their souls to their God'. At the other end of the central island in the square, a (once again, dry) drinking fountain erected by the Metropolitan Drinking Fountain and Cattle Trough Association bears the delightful but anonymous inscription: 'To a revered husband and father from his loving wife and children – 1882'.

Chelsea Physic Garden

Retrace your steps back to Royal Hospital Road. Walk southwards down the left-hand side of the road, past the National Army Museum on your left, cross Tite Street and then turn left into Swan Walk where the entrance to Chelsea Physic Garden is located. (Check the website for public 'open days' as they are few and far between. The garden remains the private property of the Society of Apothecaries.)

You have seen the newest statue of **Sir Hans Sloane** by Sloane Square (and could see the oldest in the British Museum, if the museum could find it!), so it seems only right to inspect the site and the jesmonite facsimile of the original alabaster of **Sloane [20]** as well. The garden, founded in 1673, is the second-oldest botanic garden in England, with only Oxford's garden its senior. When Sloane bought Chelsea Manor as his home in 1712, he also acquired the freehold of the garden, which he presented to the Society of Apothecaries as a gift in 1722. It was to honour his benefaction, as well as to honour one of the great physicians and botanists of the time, that the society commissioned *Rysbrack's* statue. You will meet Sloane again, as you pass Chelsea Old Church in Cheyne Row.

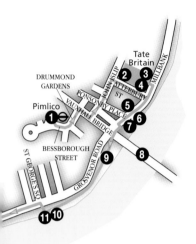

1 Air Vent
2 Sir John Everett Millais
3 The Rescue of Andromeda
4 The Death of Dirce
5 Jété
6 Mooring Stone
7 Locking Piece
8 Vauxhall Bridge
9 River Cut Tide
10 William Huskisson
11 The Helmsman
12 Memorial to the VI Dragoon Guards
13 Chilianwalla Monument
14 Charles II
15 Chelsea In-Pensioner
16 Sir Hans Sloane

17 Two Pupils of c.1814
18 Venus Fountain
19 War Memorial
20 Sloane
21 Rossetti Drinking Fountain
22 The Boy David
23 Boy with a Dolphin
24 Atalanta
25 Thomas Carlyle
26 Drinking fountain
27 Thomas More
28 Funerary urn
29 Female lower torso
30 Awakening
31 Lamp standards
32 James McNeill Whistler

Embankment Gardens/Cheyne Walk

Leave the garden, turning left up Swan Walk and then left again back on to Royal Hospital Road. At the west end of Royal Hospital Road you reach Chelsea Embankment Gardens. Bear right, entering the gardens, heading upstream. In the gardens, opposite Number 16 Cheyne Walk, stands the **Rossetti Drinking Fountain [21]**, commemorating Dante Gabriel Rossetti, extraordinary poet and painter and perhaps the best-known of the Pre-Raphaelites. He lived at Number 16 from 1862 until shortly before his death in 1882. The posthumous (1887) bronze three-quarter relief bust and upper torso is by his fellow Pre-Raphaelite *Ford Madox Brown*, the design of the fountain by *J. P. Seddon*. The distinguished list of subscribers' names on the bronze plaque on the reverse of the fountain includes Sir Lawrence Alma-Tadema, William Holman Hunt, Sir John Everett Millais and Algernon Charles Swinburne.

Near the fountain, fronting the main Embankment carriageway and unveiled posthumously in 1975, is a fibreglass replacement by *Edward Bainbridge Copnall* of **The Boy David [22]**, the original bronze of which – by *Francis Derwent Wood* – was stolen. It bears a strong resemblance to *Derwent Wood's* **Machine Gun Corps Memorial** at Hyde Park Corner (see page 31), and indeed was the model for that memorial. It too is inscribed as 'A memorial to the members of the Machine Gun Corps who served in World War I'.

At the Oakley Street junction, facing towards Albert Bridge, is *David Wynne's* 1975 bronze **Boy with a Dolphin [23]**, nicely described by Pevsner as 'quite a virtuoso piece of pop art'. Just upstream of the bridge, between the carriageway and the river, stands a bronze **Atalanta [24]**, also by *Francis Derwent Wood*. It was 'placed here in his memory [in 1929] by members of the Chelsea Arts Club and other friends'. Atalanta was the fleet-of-foot quasi-Artemis who successfully avoided matrimony by out-running all her suitors, until Hippomenes brought Aphrodite's three golden apples into play.

In the Embankment Gardens, with his back to Carlyle Mansions just behind him, is *Edgar Boehm's* 1882 bronze of **Thomas Carlyle [25]**, the essayist and historian, who lived at what is now 24 Cheyne Row for nearly fifty years until his death in 1881. Carlyle is portrayed seated, and wearing a huge overcoat that seems almost as formidable as the greatcoat on **Churchill** in Parliament Square (see page 50).

All Saints, Cheyne Row

In front of Chelsea Old Church (or more formally, All Saints, Cheyne Row) you find yet another dry commemorative **drinking fountain [26]**. The fountain itself, of 1880, is relatively unremarkable, but once again it bears a charming testimonial: 'In affectionate remembrance of the late George Sparkes of Bromley in Kent formerly judge at Madras in the East India Company's Civil Service. A great and good man gifted with every refined feeling and much esteemed by all who knew him...'

Between the fountain and the church is a curious seated statue of **Thomas More [27]** – curious because the piece is unexpressive, and is black apart from the insignia, face and hands of More, which are all picked out in gold. The statue is the 1969 work of *Leslie Cubitt Bevis*. The west and east sides of the plinth bear the words 'scholar' and 'statesman' respectively, whereas the supreme accolade 'saint' on the north side is barely visible on account of the hedge.

Here again you encounter Sloane. The most notable and conspicuous memorial in the churchyard is his **funerary urn [28]** by *Joseph Wilton*, under a small stone pavilion at the south-east corner. It bears a commemorative plaque: 'To the memory of Sir Hans Sloane Bart. President of the Royal Society and of the College of Physicians who in the year of Our Lord 1753 the 92nd of his age without the least pain of body and with a conscious serenity of mind ended a virtuous and beneficent life. This monument was erected by his two daughters Eliza Cadogan and Sarah Stanley.' On the opposite, north, side a shorter legend records: 'Here lies interred Elizabeth Lady Sloane wife of Sir Hans Sloane Bart. Who departed this life in the year of Our Lord 1724 and the 67th of her age.'

Roper's Garden

To the west of Chelsea Old Church there is a sunken, open garden. This is Roper's Garden, which was created in 1964 on the site of buildings destroyed by a parachute mine on 17 April 1941. The site of the garden formed part of the marriage gift of Thomas More to his daughter Margaret and her husband William Roper in 1521. At the east end there is a free-standing stone relief by *Jacob Epstein* of a **female lower torso [29]**. The torso faces west, upriver, and on its east side the stone bears the inscription: 'Unveiled by Admiral Sir Caspar John 3 June 1972. This carving by Jacob Epstein commemorates the years 1909–1914 when he lived and worked in a studio on this site which was originally Sir Thomas More's studio.' Caspar John himself was both son of artistic Augustus and an Admiral of the Fleet. In the middle of the garden is perhaps the most beautiful bronze nude in London – **Awakening [30]**. It is an early work by *Gilbert Ledward*, erected here to commemorate his life-long association with this quarter of Chelsea.

Embankment Commemoration

After that abundance of statuary along this short stretch of Chelsea Embankment, you should not forget the commemoration of the construction of the Embankment itself, which was completed in 1874. Two Coalbrookdale elaborate, ornamental bronze **lamp standards** [31] – one just downstream of Albert Bridge, the other on the carriageway by Chelsea Old Church – each feature two elongated conch shells spilling forth cornucopias of fruit, while two young boys climb the standard, the lower holding a burning torch to pass to the upper, to light the lamp.

In Celebration of a Painter

A few steps further to Battersea Bridge, and the last statue on this walk. Just beyond the bridge, holding sketchbook and pencil, gazing upriver along Battersea Reach, is **James McNeill Whistler** [32]. This is a 2005 bronze by *Nicholas Dimbleby*, by way of a slightly belated centennial commemoration of the death (in 1903) of the distinguished American artist and most celebrated painter of Old Battersea Bridge. He is best seen from the Embankment pavement, on the upstream side of the bridge.

From Beaufort Street, which joins the north end of Battersea Bridge, a 345 bus will take you to South Kensington Underground Station, and a 19 bus will take you to Sloane Square.

13. CANARY WHARF AND GREENWICH – FROM POSTMODERN FUTURE TO BAROQUE PAST

START	Canary Wharf Underground Station (Jubilee line) or Canary Wharf Docklands Light Railway Station
FINISH	Cutty Sark Docklands Light Railway Station
DISTANCE	4.4 km (2 ³/₄ miles) excluding train ride
DURATION	2 ½ hours

This walk is the odd one out in this book in that it includes a short railway trip and it offers the greatest contrasts of scenery – between the twenty-first century transatlantic architecture of Canary Wharf and the seventeenth- and eighteenth-century baroque splendour of Greenwich, with sculpture in both cases to match.

From central London you can travel to Canary Wharf by the Docklands Light Railway (DLR) or the Jubilee line. The DLR, a fully automated overland light railway, has transformed the accessibility of the old London docklands, with easy and rapid communications between the City, City Airport and Greenwich and, at the hub of those three furthest points, Canary Wharf. Built partly on old railway embankments and partly on new high-level tracks, the DLR is unique in inner London's railway network in providing a marvellous view of the urban landscape through which it passes – in this case, the regenerated Docklands. The underground Jubilee line comes without the panorama, but affords easy access from the West End and the opportunity to disembark at the remarkable subterranean cathedral that is Canary Wharf Underground Station – arguably the most architecturally spectacular station on the entire Underground network.

First Impressions of Canary Wharf

Canary Wharf is well signposted. Follow the signs from either the DLR or the Underground to Canada Square. Canary Wharf is extraordinary: no lesser word will suffice to begin to describe it. The name comes from the name given to the warehouse built in the early 1950s for Fred Olsen Lines on the south quay of West India Import Dock, in what was already, in retrospect, the twilight of the working life of the London docks. The West India Docks, which the modern Canary Wharf development straddles, were the first of London's purpose-built commercial docks – begun on 12 July 1800 and opened for business on 1 September 1802. Instead of lying in the Pool of London and being dependent on lighters to load and unload – a process that could take anything up to four weeks – ships could dock, in the modern sense that we know, and be turned round within four

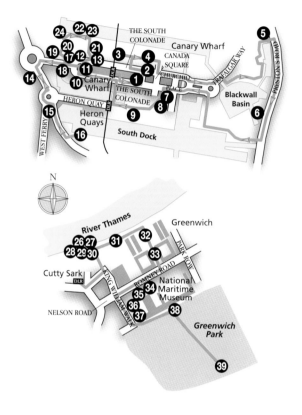

1. It Takes Two
2. Bronze Lions
3. Original Form
4. Midland Bank War Memorial
5. Figurehead for Docklands
6. Leap
7. Centaur
8. Cross Way and Arbor
9. Testa Addormenta
10. Two Men on a Bench
11. Couple on a Seat
12. Michael von Clemm
13. Returning to Embrace
14. Vanishing Point
15. Traffic Light Tree
16. Docklands Enterprise
17. Willoughby Passage Gates
18. Man with Open Arms
19. Centurione
20. Screen
21. Sculptural Railing
22. Sir Robert Milligan
23. Milligan bronze relief
24. Hibbert Gate
25. West Gates
26. Naval Heads
27. Sir Walter Ralegh
28. Turkish Bronze Gun
29. New Zealand Memorial Obelisk
30. Lewin Gates
31. Bellot Memorial
32. George II
33. Nelson Pediment
34. Thompson Memorial
35. Cemetery Monument
36. Fish
37. William IV
38. Titanic Memorial Garden
39. General Wolfe

days. For 150 years the West India Docks were at the heart of the greatest commercial port in the world, but from the 1950s decline set in. Containers and larger vessels increasingly drove shipping downriver to Tilbury or further afield to modern ports like Felixstowe. The late 1960s saw the beginning of the closure of the upriver docks, for want of trade, and the West India Docks were themselves closed in 1980.

To offset the consequent unemployment (in their heyday the West India Dock's alone had employed nearly fifty thousand men) and economic deprivation, the Conservative government of the day gave the Docklands the status of an Enterprise Zone. This was essentially an umbrella of generous tax breaks, with a view (as it was thought at the time) to regenerating light industrial activity. However, a serendipitous link of men and circumstances led to the London Docklands Development Corporation sowing the unforeseen seed of an office development and to its subsequent spectacular exploitation by the Canadian developers Olympia & York, who had previously created Battery Park in New York. Despite a serious property slump shortly afterwards, and the consequent bankruptcy of Olympia & York, the development has gone from strength to strength. It now boasts the three tallest buildings in Britain, employs over one hundred thousand people and both complements and competes with the traditional City as a major financial services centre.

Given that history, therefore, you should not be surprised, particularly if you arrive from the depths of the Jubilee line, by the impression that you have arrived in another country. Furthermore, you will feel that it looks overwhelmingly North American: skyscrapers, rectangular lines, modernity in every direction; architecture that is manifestly not English; street names such as Canada Square and Cabot Square; and 1 Canada Square, the tallest and starkest of all these office behemoths. These modern office buildings, with their unbroken lines and acres of sheer glass, do not easily lend themselves to sculptural adornment, so find instead free-standing statuary and sculpture.

For the purposes of this walk, Canary Wharf can be divided into two parts, respectively east and west of the DLR as it runs across the wharf. The east has rather more walking and less sculpture, and the west has its sculpture largely concentrated within easy reach of Cabot Square.

Canada Square

On the south side of Canada Square you find It Takes Two [1], an abstract bronze of 2002 by *Bob Allen*, of two entwined figures who are more or less life-size, if that is not a contradiction in terms in a description of an abstract work. On the north side of the square, outside the HSBC Tower skyscraper, are two Bronze Lions [2]. Cast in 2002, these are exact replicas of the original lions by *W. W. Wagstaff* cast in 1935 for the Hong Kong office of the Hongkong and Shanghai Banking Corporation, the founding member of the HSBC Group. A similar pair by *Henry Poole*, cast in 1923, for many years guarded the Shanghai office of the bank.

Waterfront

Walk a few steps to the west and down to the waterfront of the Import Dock immediately opposite 1 Canada Square. Follow the waterfront round to the left and just before the DLR crosses overhead you find *Keith Rand's* 1999 work, Original Form [3]. First impressions of a tree trunk are matched by equal first assumptions of a piece in rusting metal. In this instance, impressions are right and assumptions are wrong. It is in fact carved from the trunk of a single Douglas fir.

Retrace your steps to where you first joined the waterfront and then follow it round to the north side of the HSBC Tower. Here you meet a reminder of HSBC's 'City' history. The London Joint City and Midland Bank War Memorial [4] was first unveiled in 1921 at the Midland Bank's Threadneedle Street branch, in the heart of the City, commemorating the 717 named members of the bank's staff who gave their lives in the Great War. When the branch closed in 1992, the memorial was moved to HSBC's offices in Leadenhall Street, HSBC having by that time acquired the Midland Bank. When HSBC moved to Canary Wharf, the memorial followed, and was re-dedicated in its present location on Armistice Day 2002. In marble, with a triangular pediment and fourteen panels of names, the memorial features two bronze statues by *Albert Toft* (whose Royal Fusiliers Memorial can be seen on the walk on pages 100–9), with St George on the right and the Recording Angel on the left. Just to the right of the main Great War Memorial is the bank's separate, smaller memorial to the dead of the Second World War – a more modest bronze and glass encased Book of Remembrance.

Two Docks

From the east end of Canada Square you are going to take a fairly long walk that will give you a better idea of the perspective of the docks before the Canary Wharf development, and includes a couple more pieces of sculpture. Leave Canada Square from its top-right corner, cross Upper Bank Street and continue east to Churchill Place; continue out from its far end, and cross to the right side of the road. Continue round the grassed roundabout (ignoring the first set of steps, to which you will be returning shortly), go past the security barrier onto the bridge and take the pedestrian stairs down from the bridge onto the Blackwall Basin quayside. Walk along the north side of the Blackwall Basin and then around the perimeter of Poplar Dock, both now used by barges and pleasure craft. At the furthest, north-east corner of Poplar Dock stands the steel **Figurehead for Docklands** [5], a 1997 piece by *Anna Bisset*, part Queen Elizabeth I on her way to Tilbury to greet Sir Francis Drake, part metallic scarecrow.

Walk round the far side of the dock and on to Prestons Road, and then down to Blackwall Basin Graving Dock, which adjoins the west (inshore) side of Prestons Road. Here you find **Leap [6]** in the middle of the dock itself – eight stylized dolphins in bronze, all leaping out of the water. It is a 1982 piece by the Czech sculptor *Franta Belsky*, and is an interesting contrast with his two very much more conventional admirals, Mountbatten and Cunningham, in St James's Park and Trafalgar Square (see pages 43 and 63).

Canary Wharf

Walk a little further down Prestons Road. Turn right opposite The Gun pub, immediately before the road bridge over the entrance to West India Dock (there is a signpost indicating the pedestrian route back to Canary Wharf); follow the tarmac road along the north side of the dock, and then again when it turns sharp right; at the end of the road you will see the set of steps which you ignored on your outward journey. Climb the steps and go back round the roundabout to Churchill Place. This time, bear left, and at the crossroads turn left into Montgomery Street and then right into Montgomery Square. Ahead of you, outside the east exit from the Underground station, in Upper Bank Street, stands *Igor Mitoraj's* bronze **Centaur [7]** (see illustration, page 133)– a centaur with a semi-lopped head standing over a prone torso, with strange miniature figures set into apertures in the centaur's body. *Mitoraj* is a German-born Pole, sculpting in the classical tradition with a particular focus on the well-modelled torso, often with a postmodern twist of ostentatiously truncated limbs emphasizing the damage sustained by most genuine classical sculptures – a characteristic that will be more apparent in the second and third of his public works here at Canary Wharf.

Almost next to **Centaur** is **Cross Way and Arbor [8]**, a 2003 work by *Nigel Ross*, two overlapping pieces carved from the single trunks of a European larch and an elm.

If you then walk round the south side of Jubilee Park (the landscaped open space on whose east side stand the two previous sculptures), you meet the second of *Mitoraj's* pieces, the bronze bandaged face of **Testa Addormenta [9]**, standing outside the East Wintergarden.

Cabot Square

Proceed to the west side of Jubilee Park, and then to the north side of Middle Dock. To the west of the DLR, facing Middle Dock and at the bottom of the steps leading up to Cabot Square, is the bronze pair of **Two Men on a Bench [10]**, a 1999 bronze by *Giles Penny* of (as the name suggests) two rather charmingly rounded semi-abstract men, seated informally, back to back.

Up the steps and into the middle of Cabot Square itself, you find another bronze, **Couple on a Seat [11]** (see illustration, left). This pair is a 1984 work by *Lynn Chadwick*, with two sharply angular seated figures, very typical of the artist.

In the north-west corner of the square is a modest bronze medallion, with a bas-relief head, by *Gerald Laing* in 1998. It commemorates **Michael von Clemm [12]**, who died in 1997, described on its plinth as the 'investment banker and pioneer of the Euromarkets whose vision helped to create this financial centre'.

Outside Number 10 Cabot Square, on the north side, is *Jon Buck's* work **Returning to Embrace [13]**, a bronze with a copper-green patina from 2000, a bafflingly compact male and female couple in the most intimate, and intricate, embrace.

All Roads Lead to Westferry Circus

West India Avenue leads off the west side of Cabot Square. Walk down it towards Westferry Circus. For the visitor arriving by road, or by water and arriving at the pier on the west side of the circus, West India Avenue is the transit lounge between English London and North American Canary Wharf. At the circus itself, on the river side, is *Jay Battle's* 1999 **Vanishing Point [14]**, an oversized 1.2-metre (4-foot) diameter rough cast Polo mint with a very small hole, in Derbyshire limestone and set on a low steel plinth.

If you then briefly follow the main perimeter road south for a short distance, in the middle of the next roundabout immediately to the south of Westferry Circus, is *Pierre Vivant's* **Traffic Light Tree** [15], an outsize multiple traffic light in painted steel and lights, a 1998 work funded and produced by the Public Art Commissions Agency.

From that roundabout, proceed roughly 100 metres down Marsh Wall. Next to you at that point, in the south-west corner of South Dock, you can see *Wendy Taylor's* 1987 abstract aluminium piece entitled **Docklands Enterprise** [16].

Around West India Avenue

Retrace your steps back to Westferry Circus and walk eastwards along the north side of West India Avenue towards Cabot Square. Just before reaching the square you will pass the **Willoughby Passage Gates** [17], sculpted steel gates by *Katy Hackney*, of 2000. On the central reservation of the avenue is another work by *Giles Penny* – his 1995 **Man with Open Arms** [18] – a roughly textured bronze of a standing male figure stretching out his arms.

To the north of West India Avenue (roughly 50 metres west of the Willoughby Passage Gates) is the pedestrian piazza Columbus Courtyard. On its west side stands Canary Wharf's third bronze piece by *Igor Mitoraj*, a large neoclassical mask entitled **Centurione** [19], an early 1990s work. On the north side of the courtyard, overlooking the Import Dock, more of which in a moment, is a cut steel **Screen** [20] by *Wendy Ramshaw*, on the theme of sea navigation, with a jewelled eye as its centrepiece.

Import Dock

Not everything in Canary Wharf is spanking new and this section of the walk ends with a couple of reminders of the origins of the West India Docks. From the north side of Cabot Square, descend the steps of Wren Landing, past *Bruce McLean's* **Sculptural Railing** [21], down to the floating pontoon bridge over the Import Dock, to the remaining original warehouses along its north quay.

Number 1 Warehouse, at the west end, is now the Museum in Docklands, where the curious visitor can pause to find out a great deal more about the history of London's docks. Outside the entrance to the museum stands *Richard Westmacott's* 1812 bronze of **Sir Robert Milligan** [22], sometime chairman of the West India Company and one of the 'founding fathers' of the West India Docks. Here is the fulsome tribute, on the bronze plaque on the reverse of the pedestal, to: 'A merchant of London, to whose genius, perseverance and guardian care the surrounding great work principally owes its design, accomplishment and regulation. The directors and proprietors, deprived by his death on 21 May 1809, of the continuance of his invaluable services, by their unanimous vote have caused this statue to be erected.' On the obverse of the pedestal is a **bronze relief** [23] by *Vincent Butler*, a 1998 work based on a design of 1813 by *Westmacott* himself.

Lastly, at the west end of the Import Dock, is the **Hibbert Gate** [24]. This is a full-size replica of the original main gate to the West India Docks, erected in 2000 to mark the bicentenary of the opening of the docks. The original gateway was erected in 1805 and demolished in 1932. On top of the gate is *Leo Stevenson's* bronze model of *The Hibbert*, a typical West Indiaman, based on the Coade-stone sculpture on the original gate.

Over the River to Greenwich

So, now for the quick train ride. Proceed eastwards along the north side of the Import Dock, and you will arrive at West India Quay station. From West India Quay you quickly travel seven stations south, and three centuries back in time, to Cutty Sark DLR Station and historic Greenwich.

If you are a little more adventurous, and do not suffer from claustrophobia, leave the DLR at Island Gardens. From the bottom of Island Gardens there is a fine view across the river to the baroque splendour of the former Naval Hospital and College, which you will shortly be visiting. From the same viewing point you can take the foot tunnel under the river, emerging by the Cutty Sark on the south bank. This, the most famous of the tea clippers, is undergoing long-term restoration work, including the repair of recent and disastrous fire damage.

The complex of buildings at Greenwich is perhaps the most splendid group of baroque buildings in England and the rollcall of architects involved is about as distinguished as you can find: from *Inigo Jones*'s Queen's House, of 1620–37, which effectively replaced the earlier (and now long demolished) Tudor Greenwich Palace as a royal residence; through *John Webb*'s King Charles Block of the 1660s, which became the first part of the Naval Hospital established there in 1694 by William and Mary, after they opted for Hampton Court and Kensington Palace as royal residences in preference to Greenwich; to the later contributions of, principally, *Christopher Wren*, but also *Nicholas Hawksmoor, James Stuart* and *John Yenn*, not to mention also the ceiling of the Painted Hall by *James Thornhill*. The first naval pensioners arrived at this maritime equivalent of the Military Hospital at Chelsea in 1705. The hospital closed in 1869, to be replaced in these buildings in 1873 by the Royal Naval College, which in turn was closed in 1998, so ending three centuries' association of the Royal Navy with Greenwich. The buildings are now largely occupied by the former polytechnic, now called the University of Greenwich, and by Trinity College of Music.

The Naval Hospital and College, and the Queen's House, can more than occupy the visitor in their own right. In addition, however, the complex of buildings immediately to the west of the Queen's House now houses the National Maritime Museum, which is the country's premier naval museum. And up the slope, in the middle of Greenwich Park, is the building that has given rise to Greenwich's most widespread and enduring renown – the Royal Observatory, through which the Prime Meridian passes.

Begin at the **West Gates [25]**, which were moved to their present position (a short walk eastwards from either the dock or the foot tunnel) in 1850 from their original position just to the west of King William's and King Charles' blocks. On the two pillars are the celestial and terrestrial globes, with meridian and latitude lines inlaid in copper, designed by the mathematics master of the Greenwich Academy, *Richard Oliver*. Each globe weighs almost 7 tons.

Around the Pepys Building

Turning away from the West Gates towards the river, you find the *Cutty Sark* to your left, and to your right the entrance to the Greenwich Gateway Visitor Centre, in the former Pepys Building. Along the front of the Pepys Building are thirteen **Naval Heads [26]** – the heads of thirteen of the most illustrious of the Royal Navy's admirals and captains in the two centuries or so from Lord Howard of Effingham, who commanded the first Queen Elizabeth's fleet against the Spanish Armada of 1588, to Nelson and Trafalgar in 1805, with Anson, Drake, Cook, Blake, Benbow, Sandwich, Rodney, Duncan, Collingwood, Howe and St Vincent in between.

To the left of the entrance to the Pepys Building as you face it stands **Sir Walter Ralegh** [27] (see illustration, above), the great Elizabethan soldier, sailor, courtier, explorer, author and adventurer (he is not known to have used the spelling 'Raleigh' which appears on the plinth). He is known to generations of schoolchildren for spreading his cloak over a puddle for Queen Elizabeth I to walk on, but is more substantively renowned for being the principal founder of the first English colony 'beyond the seas', Virginia (named after the virgin queen), even though he himself never went there, and then for his long imprisonment in the Tower of London as an implacable enemy of James I and his eventual execution in 1618. This very delightful life-size bronze by *William McMillan*, of 1959, stood for many years in Whitehall, until it was moved here in 2001.

To the right of the entrance is the **Turkish Bronze Gun [28]**, which was captured by Admiral Sir John Duckworth when he took a fleet into the Sea of Marmara and on to Constantinople in 1807. Cast in 1791, it weighs 5.2 tons and fired a shot of 56 kilograms (123 pounds). It was presented to the Royal Naval Asylum at Greenwich later that year by HRH Prince Ernest Augustus, Duke of Cumberland (the fifth son of George III), and the decorative plaques of the carriage commemorate British naval victories. The asylum was subsequently absorbed into the Hospital School, and when the school moved from Greenwich to Holbrook in Suffolk (the former school buildings are now occupied by the Maritime Museum), the gun went with the school. The gun was returned here in 2007, nicely marking the bicentenary of its original arrival.

To complete the tour from this same spot, two further memorials lie between us and the river. The more conspicuous is the **New Zealand Memorial Obelisk [29]**, 'Erected by the surviving [naval] officers and men to the memory of their comrades who fell in action in New Zealand during the years 1863–1864' in one of the long succession of Maori Wars of the nineteenth century.

Beyond the obelisk are the **Lewin Gates [30]**, a discreet memorial to Admiral of the Fleet Lord Lewin, who was Chief of the Defence Staff during the Royal Navy's most memorable foray since the Second World War, the Falklands Campaign of 1982, and who died in 1999.

Old Royal Naval College

Moving east along the waterfront towards the Old Royal Naval College, you find another obelisk, the **Bellot Memorial [31]**, 'To the intrepid young Bellot of the French Navy who in the endeavour to rescue Franklin shared the fate and the glory of that illustrious navigator – from his British admirers – 1853'. The 'Franklin' in question is Sir John Franklin, who met a fatal end to his expedition to find the elusive North-West Passage in 1845 (see page 39).

In the central forecourt, between King Charles' and Queen Anne's Blocks and directly facing the river, stands *John Michael Rysbrack*'s **George II [32]**, a very weathered 1735 marble of the king in classical dress. This was the product of an early and imaginative exercise in fund-raising by the then governor of the hospital, which was in some financial difficulty. Rather than proceed with *Wren*'s plans for statues of William and Mary, the governor – Admiral Jennings – commissioned this statue of the then reigning monarch. The King was so pleased by it that he conferred on the hospital the confiscated estates of the Jacobite Earl of Derwentwater. Sadly, like George II's other statue in Golden Square (see page 55), the marble is not in the best of health.

King William's Block

Walking away from the river towards the Queen's House, you pass between the chapel to the left and the Painted Hall to the right, both of which are recommended, but are outside the scope of this walk. Then turn to the right into the inner courtyard of King William's Block, where you will see the **Nelson Pediment [33]** above the colonnade. In Coade stone, by *Benjamin West* in 1812, it depicts Britannia receiving the corpse of Nelson from a Triton at the command of Neptune, with a watching lion bearing the roll of Nelson's battles.

Greenwich Park

Proceeding away from the river towards the Queen's House, you will meet and cross Romney Road and turn right, towards the National Maritime Museum. As you enter Greenwich Park by the museum gate, however, turn towards Devonport House to the right of the museum and proceed into the enclosed garden in front of it, which is the site of the former burial ground of the old hospital. In the corner of the garden nearest the museum are the remains of the **Thompson Memorial [34]** – a broken column commemorating Vice-Admiral Sir Thomas Thompson, Bart., who as one of Nelson's captains commanded *Leander* at the Battle of the Nile and *Bellona* at Copenhagen, where he lost a leg. Subsequently he was Comptroller of the Navy, Member of Parliament for Rochester and finally Treasurer of the Hospital, in which office he died aged sixty-two in 1828. Thompson's defence of the fifty-gun *Leander* against the French seventy-four *Généreux* on 18 August 1798, when he had to strike his colours, was described at his subsequent court martial as deserving of every praise his country and the court could give, for 'his gallant and almost unprecedented defence of the *Leander* against so superior a force', and earned him both his knighthood and an annual pension of £200.

In the middle of the garden, the **Cemetery Monument [35]** – a stone pedestal, bearing a lopped obelisk, topped by Britannia – bears the legend: 'Erected by order of the Lords Commissioners of the Admiralty, 1892, In memory of the gallant officers and men of the Royal Navy and Marines to the number of about 20,000 formerly inmates of the Royal Hospital Greenwich whose remains were interred in this cemetery between the years 1749 and 1869.'

Just before you start the long walk uphill towards the Royal Observatory, make a very brief diversion to inspect the curious bronze **Fish [36]** in the residential courtyard on the west side of Devonport House, off King William Walk, a 2003 piece by *Francois Hameury* from Brittany, commissioned by Cathredal Group PLC, the developer of the surrounding flats.

To your left, at the south end of King William Walk as you are about to enter the park proper, you see the garden that is the site of the former St Mary's Church, built in 1823 and demolished in 1936. In that latter year, *Samuel Nixon*'s substantial granite statue of **William IV [37]** was re-erected here in place of the church. The statue had first been erected in 1845, at the junction of King William and Gracechurch Streets and Eastcheap, in the City, but by the 1930s London's ever-increasing traffic militated irresistibly in favour of a new pedestrian subway at that major junction. The subway could not have supported the 20 tons of statue and its supporting plinth, and a new home was required for **Sailor Billy**, the most nautical of all British monarchs, with his fellow serving sailors James II, George V and George VI as runners-up. (The Royal Navy owes its privileged tradition of remaining seated to drink the Loyal Toast to William IV.) Greenwich, with its long naval history, provided a serendipitous solution to the rehousing problem and here **Sailor Billy** has stood ever since, even if the Navy itself has now departed.

Leave Sailor Billy's Garden, turn left, or east, and follow the edge of the park until you reach the small **Titanic Memorial Garden [38]** immediately to the south of the National Maritime Museum. A simple bronze plaque on a low plinth in the flowerbed reads: 'To commemorate the sinking of RMS Titanic on 15 April 1912 and all those who were lost with her – 15 April 1995.' It was officially opened by Mrs Edith Haisman who, as a fifteen-year-old, had been a survivor of the disaster.

From the Titanic Memorial Garden, you can see your final objective. Make the long climb up the hill to the observatory and the statue of **General Wolfe [39]**. James Wolfe was one of the most remarkable of Britain's eighteenth-century generals. Even before his appointment at the tender age of thirty-two to command the 1759 expedition to Quebec, which contributed to the successful culmination of the Seven Years' War, Wolfe's brilliance had attracted the approval of George II and prompted the King's aphorism in reply to the Duke of Newcastle's complaint that Wolfe was mad: 'Mad is he? Then I hope he will *bite* some of my other generals.' His celebrated victory over the Marquis de Montcalm's French forces on the Heights of Abraham secured Quebec and Canada for Britain, and like Nelson he was immortalized by his death on the very field of his success. The obverse of the pedestal bears the simple legend 'The Victor of Quebec', and it was therefore the most elegant of graceful gestures that the statue should have been unveiled on 5 June 1930 by the then Marquis de Montcalm, the descendant of Wolfe's vanquished adversary. (By a nice coincidence, Britain's tribute to one of France's greatest twentieth-century generals, **Maréchal Foch**, was unveiled on the same day by the Prince of Wales, see page 26).

Wolfe's 2.7-metre (9-foot) bronze, by *Robert Tait Mackenzie*, stands on its substantial pedestal a few yards to the east of the observatory, and is therefore unique in all these walks as being the only statue to the east of the Prime Meridian. It also enjoys undoubtedly the best vantage point of any London statue, with the immediate contrasts of old Greenwich and new Canary Wharf laid out before your feet, and the 'ships towers domes theatres and temples' of central London dotting the western skyline, 'all bright and glittering in the smokeless air'. It is a far cry and a long haul from Westminster Bridge, where two hundred years ago the view of London prompted the poet William Wordsworth to write those words in his poem 'Composed Upon Westminster Bridge', but the poem's opening lines perhaps remain as true of the view from Greenwich today: 'Earth has not anything to show more fair: dull would he be of soul who could pass by a sight so touching in its majesty'.

To return to Cutty Sark DLR station, walk south down The Avenue, which runs into King William Walk. Turn left into College Approach and across Greenwich Church Street.

INDEX OF SCULPTORS AND ARCHITECTS

• The numbers in the right-hand column correspond with the numbers in the main text. For example: 'Maj-Gen Sir Charles Napier – 5[19]' is statue 19 in walk 5.
• Buildings and places, as opposed to sculpture and monuments, appear in italics, as do objects that are located outside the scope of these walks.
• Buildings, places and objects appearing in the right-hand column with merely a single number, e.g. 'Portland Place – 6', are mentioned in the corresponding walk, i.e. walk 6, but do not have individual numbers and are not identified on the maps.
• The particular responsibility of each artist for the corresponding work – e.g., whole or part, sculpture or architecture – is described in the text rather than in this index.
• Where the work appears in brackets, it is a copy of the original.
• Dates for the lives of individual sculptors and architects have been supplied where possible.

Walking London's Statues and Monuments

INDEX OF WORKS

• The numbers in the middle column correspond with the numbers in the main text. For example, Achilles is statue 6 in walk 1.
• Buildings and places, as opposed to sculpture and monuments, appear in italics, as do objects that are located outside the scope of these walks.
• Buildings, places and objects appearing with merely a single number in the middle column, e.g. *Belgrave Square* – 2, are mentioned in the corresponding walk, i.e. walk 2, but do not have individual numbers and are not identified on the maps.
• The particular responsibility of each artist for the corresponding work, e.g. whole or part, sculpture or architecture, is described in the text rather than in this index.
• Where the artist's name appears in brackets, the corresponding work is a copy of that artist's original.

ACKNOWLEDGEMENTS

I would particularly like to thank: John Thorn, without whose encouragement this book would not have been begun; Sally Milligan, for her collaboration, research, energy and initiative, without which the book could not have been written; and my wife Sarah, without whose essential and invaluable support it would not have been completed.